I first noticed my breasts starting to grow when I was about 13 and I can remember the day when I looked at myself in a tight top and could see their shape and felt proud. They were a double A, the same size as my friend Jennifer's. Then they started to grow and they grew and grew and now they're much bigger than hers. I'm a 34C/D and my breasts are among the biggest in my year.

Helen Hines worked for the National Council for One Parent Families Information Team for seven years before editing *Family Fallout: Young Women Talk About Family Break Up* (Livewire, 2000). She was so inspired by the experience of working with young women that she approached The Women's Press with the idea for this book.

Helen is also a published travel writer, writes songs and poetry and has run a number of writing workshops, including several in schools in North London and a regular writing group at Walthamstow School for Girls.

Helen is a director of Outlook, a personal development training company that empowers people of all ages to develop their self-confidence and live their dreams. In her spare time she loves to paint, and occasionally works as an illustrator and muralist. She has also somehow made time to take on a post-graduate psychology course at Guildhall University.

perfect

Young Women Talk about Body Image

Helen Hines, editor

Livewire

First published by Livewire Books, The Women's Press Ltd, 2002
A member of the Namara Group
34 Great Sutton Street, London EC1V 0LQ

www.the-womens-press.com

British Library Cataloguing-in-Publication Data
A catalogue record for this book is available from the British Library.

ISBN 0 7043 4983 3

Typeset in 12/14pt Bembo by FiSH Books, London
Printed and bound in Great Britain by Cox & Wyman, Reading,
Berkshire

For Mum, Sarah and Teresa

Acknowledgements

I'm very proud of all the contributors who made it into this book and grateful to all the young women who gave me an insight into their lives, including those who aren't in the book. A big thank you to the teachers who helped me set up writing groups Debbie Upton and Basman Zora — and to all the parents and teachers who encouraged young women to write. Thank you to Teresa for holding a very busy fort while I took time for this book! And to Mum for helping me with mailouts. And finally to Charlotte and Essie at The Women's Press who have been a constant source of inspiration and support.

Contents

Introduction

Perfect. Is that how you would describe your looks? The chances are you couldn't bring yourself to – modesty wouldn't permit it for a start, and what about all those imperfections (spots, blemishes, lumps and bumps) that we're programmed to look out for? The ones we constantly examine ourselves for when we look in the mirror?

When we see our reflections most of us have at least a nagging doubt that we're too fat or too thin, too tall or too short, our hair's too frizzy, or our proportions aren't right – our bum's too big and our boobs are too small, or our tummy sticks out but we have no bum. Believe it or not, most young women have ideas like this about themselves, even the really beautiful, popular ones. My personal obsession, along with lots of other women, is thinking that I'm too fat. I've thought this ever since I was at junior school but it's helped me to discover that there are other people who feel the same or that they have different obsessions. I was amazed when I found out that one friend thinks she's too thin (it's possible to be too thin?!) and that another friend is really proud of her big boobs.

In this collection teenagers get a chance to talk back about what's important to them about their looks. Some take a light-hearted look at problems like spots or questions of fashion. Others say what it's like when the going gets tough and describe life with eating disorders such as anorexia and bulimia, or times when they feel they have to cut themselves.

Growing into a woman, developing breasts and choosing whether to wear feminine clothes is another subject close to many girls' hearts. Not all young women look or feel feminine, but some are desperate to look as feminine as possible, to prove themselves as women and to be attractive to boys. Others just want to be themselves and do the things they enjoy, like participating in sports, regardless of their image.

Lots of young women find out how their image comes across to other people while they're at school. If you've been called names at school – fatty, drainpipe, speccy, ginger – you might feel there's all the more reason to think that you don't look right. Name-calling and bullying can contribute to self-doubt; in Emma's piece she describes how it got so bad that she developed agoraphobia.

As a teenager what you wear may be one of the few ways in which you can really make a statement about who you are in the world. A number of the contributors have looked at ways of expressing individuality – clothes, piercings, tattoos or hair styles. Making a stand against designer clothes, or choosing to wear or adapt the traditional clothes of their culture, or wearing clothes that express rebellion – all are statements to the world about who these teenagers are on the inside. Sarah points out that not only does she want to be able to express her individuality through her clothes, she also wants others to accept her for the image that she projects through these clothes. For others it is more important to fit in, to be fashionable, to keep up with the Joneses. One thing you can be sure of though is that everyone wants to be accepted.

I asked some of the contributors to describe what the perfect woman would look like. Many pointed out that the most attractive feature a person can have is self-confidence. Here are some of their words: 'a perfect-looking woman is one who is...full of confidence, and laughter, and elegance, and a radiance that comes from within', 'who looks truly happy', 'confident-looking', 'one who looks like she is happy with herself...and who knows that looking good is more a matter of attitude than looks'.

Ade, one of the contributors to this book, was lucky to have her auntie Yinka around when she was growing up. 'She always told me...how beautiful and intelligent [I was], and what you hear determines how you think. She just made me feel good about myself from an early age and that has been with me and will be for the rest of my life.'

So self-esteem is an important part of self-image; if you feel confident you'll look in the mirror and be pleased with what you see, you'll walk with your head held high and with a smile in your step. You'll have a look in your eye and a mantra in your mind that says, like the T-shirt in Wessen's piece, 'I look so good I could eat myself'.

On the other hand, if you don't feel confident you might be a Jennifer Anniston look-alike but still no great shakes in your own eyes because your boobs are too big or your hips too narrow. And what about the girl that everyone agrees looks great? Do you think she's never affected by jealousy from other girls who envy her? She might have a Kate Moss figure, but there's bound to be something about her appearance that she doesn't like. She might think she's too thin or too fat; she might even have anorexia nervosa. Gaining self-confidence can be easier said than done, so if you're struggling with it, don't give up. Remember that we're all in the same boat.

I've got a friend called Saskia who used to be a top model in The Netherlands. Until a couple of years ago she regularly modelled clothes in glossy magazines. She's tall, slim, blonde and has the most amazing cheek bones. She told me that the absolute essentials for a perfect model are good bone structure, clear skin and height – the perfect height for the catwalk and magazines is 5 foot 10½. And of course, a model must be thin. In fact there's a scale of thinness for different types of modelling: catalogues want girls who are thin, not skinny; magazines only use the very skinny; fashion shows even skinnier; and for haute couture, the model should be almost falling apart. She told me that most models would be delighted if 'the perfect shape' was a little bigger, because there are really not that many full-grown women who are naturally that skinny!

Over the last few years the model image has become even thinner. About fifteen years ago, the average model was rounder and wholesome looking, with a pout, a big smile, and curves. Some models even stuffed socks or silicon bags in their bras to give themselves boobs. Nowadays, the flat chest is in.

4

Like most models, Saskia had to deal with a lot of pressure to maintain her very slim figure. At one fashion show casting she was told she had a problem with her hips, implying that her bottom was too big. She stormed out shouting, 'No I don't! You have a problem with my hips. And please don't make it mine!' She proudly walked away, but still couldn't resist the temptation to jump on the scales as soon as she got home.

So, even 'the perfect people' aren't perfect. Not according to other people's judgements anyway.

Or you could say that everyone's perfect, just different. Isn't it amazing that no two faces, of all the billions of faces in the world, are the same? Think about it – every single face is different, and every body is different too. So who's to say who is good looking, beautiful, the right shape and size or perfect? You decide.

Helen Hines

Well

Sam Lyon

Being well again feels like swimming to the surface of a deep dark lake and taking that first breath of fresh air. It's like the wonderful sense of accomplishment a mountain climber achieves when reaching the top of a peak or like being held close to someone with whom you feel completely safe. Now that I've recovered from my eating disorder I feel that my life has been given back to me, wrapped up in beautiful ribbons.

My eating disorder began, in my opinion, due to pressure. Pressure from my parents, pressure from other members of my family and pressure to do well at school. My parents wanted me to be special and to grow up quickly. My mum wanted me to take every opportunity that came my way. She had already decided, when I had just turned 14, that I was headed for the best local college, despite the extra entry requirements. Academically I was achieving and doing the best I could, but the pressure to succeed was more than I could handle. I just didn't know what level of work was required to get into this college.

My new Saturday job was another source of pressure around this time. My nan found me the job in a bakery and, eager for a challenge and some money in my pocket, I was overjoyed. This was my chance to grow up. I would enter the adult world, something that both excited and frightened me. But it soon became clear that something wasn't right. The shop only had one till and adding up a bill in my head for an impatient mother with young children, or the old gentleman who desperately wanted to leave our crowded shop, made me flustered. I managed to kid myself that the job was OK, that every week was another chance to prove that I could do what they had asked of me, but in reality every week was a new humiliation. For the first time in my life I could not fulfil people's expectations of me. It hurt, and this seemed to trigger off my insecurities.

The announcement that I had failed the month trial period at the bakery felt like a punch in the face. I was suddenly shown that adults could be cruel, that their world was scary and hurried and not something that I wanted to enter.

I spent a few days job-hunting before I told my mum that I had lost the job. She was clearly disappointed in me. Everyone in my family knew about it and whenever I brought up the subject I was told that I should be disappointed by what I had done. My grandparents reacted by throwing sums at me whenever we met so I took to avoiding them as much as possible.

Between them, my family put a huge amount of pressure on me to find another job. But try as I might there were simply none to be had in Wellington, the small town where I live, and it was only a matter of time before my self-hatred started to emerge.

I began to turn to food, eating chocolate, sandwiches and sweets all the time, as a means of muting the powerful feelings I was feeling. This drove my mum to distraction. She's always said that I should never be fat because I can see in her the repercussions of eating too much. She is bigger than some people – size 16 – and she was always counting the calories in what she ate. In my opinion she's not really what people would ordinarily class as large. I think that she's a very beautiful woman.

I started to feel fat and that my legs were very big: short and wide. I thought that I took up a lot of space. When I looked in the mirror I didn't think my body was like anybody else's – it was wrong, a big mistake. It didn't feel like it was mine, it felt alien and I thought I was fatter than everyone else. When I was going through a particularly troubled time I would see myself as fatter. Every problem put weight on me in my eyes and mind.

At the time I was pouring my heart out to my diary.

Tuesday 21 March 2000
I am scared, scared that I'm eating too much, and scared that I am ill. Eating makes my stomach ache and my whole body sick inside. It makes me feel dizzy with thoughts that aren't mine.

This was the beginning. The next day I got up and ate nothing. Then the following day, and the day after. For four days I ate nothing. When I did allow myself to eat it was an orange and a mouthful of peas; they were painful to eat, both emotionally and physically. Not eating was like reaching a state of perfection, so when I did eat it was almost like I was contaminating myself. I was crying inwardly, if not outwardly. I was crying a lot at that time.

I knew I couldn't keep up just not eating, so I began to binge eat, mostly after school. I became very scared of becoming bigger so almost immediately I found myself trying to relieve my body of the food I had eaten. I would lean over the toilet, scratching at the back of my throat, hoping that this time it would work. It wasn't always successful although I am still unsure why, but my tearful attempts were relentless.

I felt very lonely at this point and found it particularly difficult to eat with other people. I wanted to be alone but I also wanted to tell others about what was going wrong in my life, to scream it out. I'd get so hungry and then I'd eat really quickly and feel disgusting. On the few occasions I was sick I felt such an overwhelming freedom. It was like I was purifying my whole body of the toxins I had put into it and getting rid of other things along with the food. It was as if I'd achieved something. And, more than anything else in the world, I wanted to do it again and again.

Along with the food I felt like I was also getting rid of derogatory remarks or comments that had unintentionally upset me. Like when my best friend said 'Oh I can't deal with your eating problem and I don't want to be your best friend if you're going to do that.' She'd be quite sarcastic even while trying to encourage me to stop vomiting, hinting that if I valued her as a friend I'd stop it. Looking back I could see it was too much for her to handle but at the time I was really upset. In a way I agreed with her; she was just expressing what I was thinking anyway. She told other people without asking if I minded. She said she did it to find out what they thought about my problem but the news spread to lots of people I wasn't friends with. Despite this difficult time, she and I are still quite close friends. At the end of the day she was the best friend I had and I wanted her approval.

Tuesday 21 March 2000

I wish at this moment that someone would hug me. I know that when I stop writing I will be alone in my bed, when I turn the light out I will still be alone, and tomorrow at school I will be even more alone, because I will not even be able to sort things out in my own head.

I felt my friends had drifted and things became even worse still. In desperation I began to self-harm by scratching myself with my nails, making gouges on my arms, legs and stomach. Hurting myself made the cold, numb feeling go away and it was like a punishment for eating. I used the pain to blackmail myself to eat less and although it worked at first I was concerned that my eating problem would escalate.

My school work was suffering, too. My starvation meant that I'd feel too cold and tired to concentrate in class and was too tired to do any homework. I've always been one of the best in class – one of the top four – so to not be able to put my best into it was very difficult for me.

My recovery began the second I told my mum. Well, actually, I was rumbled: she noticed the scratches on my hand and made me explain how they had come about. Having no other explanation I began to tell her the truth. Many tears were shed that evening.

Friday 24 March 2000

Mum spoke to Mrs Barnes (my geography teacher) about me today. I said I didn't mind because I thought I'd find it reassuring that my teacher knew but then she told all the staff and I feel like people are talking about me on every corner. I can't look any of my teachers straight in the face any more. I'm not crazy or some kind of mental case, am I?

Then my doctor arranged some counselling for me. I was in two minds about going ahead with it and was really frightened. The only reason that I agreed to it was because I didn't think that Mum and I could sort it out on our own.

Thursday 6 April 2000

I was nervous at the counselling meeting this afternoon, but it went much better than I had anticipated. There is still a lot I feel we need to discuss; for example we never spoke about the scratches on my arms, legs and stomach. I guess I can mention this next time. I'm not sure whether to allow my counsellor to read this diary or not; it raises a lot of things that I would like to talk about, but don't feel able to say.

My counsellor made a point of not talking about my eating; he was more interested in the causes of my problems with it and side-effects of it.

Mum monitored my eating and made sure I had my evening meal. At lunchtime I usually ate my sandwich, although I scraped the butter off. I kept a calorie chart in the back of my diary. I thought I was better at different stages and managed to convince an awful lot of people that I was, but then what I'd write in my diary would be different.

Sunday 14 May 2000

I went out today wearing a skirt. I thought this was a good way to make a fresh start, but it turned out to be a huge mistake. I felt that everyone was looking at my legs with their grotesque fatness and their scarring. I can't do this again. Walking home from my best friend's house on my own was a nightmare; I was nearly in tears.

I wrote more in the later diaries about how I was feeling and this helped to get things out, rather than starving myself or being sick.

I had a brilliant pen pal, Cindy, in America who understood everything I was going through because she'd had bulimia for thirteen years. If any feelings of anxiety started coming back I'd contact her. She's a little star! I met her through the internet, which is a phenomenal resource where you can meet people in similar situations.

As I recovered I felt I was real again, rather than on my own and away from everyone else. I started to realise how lucky I was that I had my family's love and attention.

Today I am working and I feel completely secure in what I do. I waitress with people I love and I have even begun to use the till on odd occasions. The other staff are aware of the difficulties that I have. They take an interest in my written work and schooling, which has given me the confidence boost I so badly needed to aid my quest to get well.

Now I'm a lot more confident and feel like it's OK to be me. I don't count calories anymore. I am a vegetarian and eat healthily; it's important to me that I have some control over my food. Not eating meat makes me feel good because I'm avoiding the chemicals that go into it.

I've done well in my GCSEs and got into the college that my mum wanted me to go to, which has been a big boost to me. When I look at myself I'm happy with what I see. It seems that society wants you to be under-confident but I think that's pants, I think you should be overconfident.

Looking back, in a funny way I'm glad that it happened because of what it taught me about myself. I think my experiences have made me a much more compassionate and loving person. I was ill for about six months and then recovering for another six months. I hope that I can perhaps restore the faith of those in the same situation; that there is help, there is love, that each person has their own spark and it doesn't matter if they're fat, thin or indifferent. Good luck.

Colour

Ade Atayero

To me, fashion is personal. What I wear reflects my nature and culture. I'm positive and I've got attitude and determination. My bold clothes show this to the world. I'm also of Nigerian origin and I like to wear the styles that reflect my tradition. I like to see individuality in what people wear; after all there's more to clothes than how much you paid for them and whether a designer made them. Whatever you choose to wear, I think the most important thing is that you find your own style.

My African outfits, for example, reflect the fact that I'm a very colourful person. Some people think I'm crazy to be walking down the street in African wear, instead of those over-priced designer labels. But I don't care! To me it's a pride thing. I mean, I have a culture I'm damn well proud of, so why not show how we dress and how good we look? People at school or even family members sometimes try and tell me that I'm no longer in Nigeria; you know, the whole 'when in Rome do as the Romans do'? But what if I don't exactly like how the Romans do?

Y'know who inspired me to start loving African stuff? My best friend. She's Asian and her name is Shabana Nafis. She's always wearing her shalwar kameez to school and at work, wherever. I asked her one day how she feels when people stare at her because of how she dresses. She told me she didn't care, and it was a choice. She's proud of her Asian culture and dressing in this way maintains cultural dignity; she's different and special! That made me think that although I'm now in the western world, I can still hold on to my culture – well, some parts of it. Besides, I always look real good in Afro attire! When I come into school people can tell me apart from everyone else. My friends who are of African origin think I have plenty of guts for being able to walk down the street in my clothes. Yeah, I might, but it's not about guts.

I can't always dress African (thanks to the weather). Nigeria is a hot country and the clothes from there are made for summer not winter, so I can't wear them as often as I'd like. Don't get me wrong, I do love American/black British style clothes. Whatever I'm wearing I like to stand out and I hate wearing dull clothes. If I'm in jeans or a suit I'll go for bright colours; – if it's red, it has to be bright red, yellow has to be yellow and not a dull orange. God put colours in nature, right? So why not wear them to thank Him for it. Also, in Nigeria, those who wear black in their clothes are mourners. So unless you are a vicar there's no reason to wear black all the time. Despite my love for colours, I always try to balance them, or match them. Like, I don't go out with browns and greens in the same outfit (ugh!). Colours should either match (blue and white) or contrast (red and green). I may not be an artist but I think so far

I've done fine. My colours are bold and not everyone can wear them like I do.

The type of traditional clothes I wear are not typically Yoruba, which is the culture I come from. My style is borrowed from the Hausa culture and sometimes from other countries like Ghana and Sierra Leone. It's usually a fitted skirt and blouse. My favourite outfit of all time is yellow with leaf prints on it, with some light green material on the odd side. It's a really long fitted gown with short sleeves, a long skirt of the same print and a head tie as well. I think it's so beautiful!

The western world categorises people size-wise: you're either a size 6, 8, 10 and so on but you can never be in between. I'm a size 11 so I have to buy either 10 or 12; 10 is too tight and 12 is too loose, so either I look like my lungs are the size of a raisin, or like I just ate the whole of Sainsbury's. That's the beauty of my African wear: it's made to your fit and your preference, so you get value for money. You can choose your own style and size, and even the fabrics are not pre-chosen. You can actually get a whole tailor-made collection that fits you personally, without being conned into buying certain stuff that you will never wear again. You might be thinking 'Oh, so everyone in Nigeria is so rich they can have clothes custom made?' No! That's just the way it is. You can't pre-sew these clothes because no one ever has the same exact measurement.

When it comes to choosing what to wear, I always have the final say. My mom rarely comes to find me in a 'oh my gosh I don't know what to wear today' crisis. I remember one time she wanted me to wear my 'Afro attire' and I was, like, 'HELL NO!' I gave her a million and ten reasons and, surprisingly, she didn't push it. I think the reason I didn't want to was that I was going into a new environment and the last thing I wanted to do was to stick out like a sore thumb. I just wanted to blend in and be a regular Jane (plus I was going through a rather difficult time in my life and I didn't want to draw more attention to myself). I needed to let someone else take the reins of life for a while. Turns out now that I'm the one wanting to wear these clothes and she's giving me those 'I told you so' looks.

My clothes and colours are sometimes mood revealers; from days when my energy level is, like, awesome, to days when I'm so ticked off I feel like a clock, my colours show it. Although it's not all the time; sometimes I could be feeling just normal and people might think I'm so happy I could bounce to the moon 'cos of how I look. By nature I'm a very happy and annoyingly positive person. I see good and promise in everything, although that's not all the time.

My friends sometimes think that I'm vain because I see my reflection in a mirror and I'm smiling and going 'Damn! God really put His best into this fine face of mine.' That's not being vain, it's being realistic! Why put myself down when I know that no one else has my face, it's for me, myself and I. I'm just appreciating the beauty in nature — that's all really. I started thinking this way because I grew up with pretty strong women around me, like my grandmother and my mom's younger sister Auntie Yinka. She always told me how special I was and how beautiful and intelligent, and what you hear determines how you think. She just made me feel good about myself from an early age and that has been with me and will be for the rest of my life.

My friends sometimes influence my decisions when I go shopping with them. But I don't like conforming to how I'm expected to look just because someone has set standards for my life; what's hot and what's not in fashion. Most people expect all teenagers to be designer-label freaks who don't appreciate the value of anything else but I wish someone would hand those teenagers a reality check. They seem to think that all there is to life is the latest Nikes or designer clothes. Most teenagers are suckers for what's cool and keeping ahead of the fashion game, so they spend all their money on things that will go out of style in the next six months.

For me it's about who you are as a person and how you choose to develop yourself. I ain't gonna be a teenager forever and, while I am, if all I can think about is building up an array of Nike trainers and CK clothes, then I'd see myself as as useless as those items will be in twenty years time. What makes a home-made shirt of less value than one made by Dolce and Gabanna? Simply 'cos it has D&G sewn on it does it mean it deserves my money? It's not about the clothes, they don't make you; its how you wear them and who you are that shows.

Now that you understand my point of view you can stop wondering why I look a certain way, and just understand that how I choose to look is a personal preference. Same goes for everyone. I may not like the way you look, but I'll respect you for being true to yourself, especially if you're not hiding behind a facade of designer clothes and accessories. So don't always try to fit in, you're perfect the way you are.

Unique

Melissa Reardon

I've never been particularly enamoured with my body. Being female is too much hassle, far too high maintenance!

I come from a mixed-race family (my dad is black and my mum white) and have a rather bizarre combination of their physical characteristics. My skin is very pale and white like my mother's but my hair is like my dad's, very dark with an almost Afro-like texture, which is fine on my head (I even dye my hair a shade darker so it is as black as black can be) but not exactly what you want on the rest of your body. I have always been incredibly paranoid about what I see as my overly hairiness and on a night out spend ages in the bath rigorously making sure I've got rid of most of it. The worst, or most noticeable, thing is the dark hair on my upper lip. Every day when I wake up the first thing I do is to get out the tweezers and pluck my eyebrows and anything noticeable on my lip. It annoys me immensely because if my skin were a shade or two darker no one would notice!

Of course, when I was younger it didn't help having an incredibly attractive and popular younger sister. She was always the beautiful one and I had to settle for being clever. We both resented each other and, in a way, still do. She is tall, slim and very good-looking. Everything I have never been. And she is beautiful in that classic mixed-race way; think Mariah Carey or Dina Carroll and you get the idea. I am not noticeably mixed race and can easily just pass as white. Friends have said there is something exotic about me, though I tend to think it is just the over-the-top eyeliner!

I sometimes feel that I am just not black enough for my father's side of the family and I don't conform to the Afro-Caribbean culture of dressing nicely and smartly like my sister does. My father is always buying me smart clothes at Christmas in an attempt to make me look better, although I always manage to twist them to fit in with my own style. My sister and I have very different personalities and very different styles that have developed as a result of our rivalry. Sometimes I don't think my father realises this. We try – consciously or not! – to look completely different from each other. My mum is far more used to my individual look and has even been known to wear my clothes when I am bored of them and have thrown them out. I share her sense of the outrageous. I always wear shoes and boots with huge heels or platform soles (my favourite platforms have springs through them) because I think I am short compared to my sister. My mum is short, too, which always makes me feel more secure.

It wasn't until I reached 18 and started attracting boyfriends (at last!) that I became even slightly comfortable with my appearance. I know it sounds shallow, but my looks are very important to me. I can't leave the house without wearing eyeliner, some strange-coloured lipstick and decent clothes. I think what has given me more confidence has been developing my own style. Call it a mishmash of goth, indie, little girl and plain freak – it's me. And attention grabbing. I get noticed. I like it. It has only really been since I came to university that I've expressed myself this way. I got involved with the local rock and metal music scene and I fit in. Nobody I tend to go out with dresses conventionally, which is very different to back home.

My new fixation now is body adornments. I've had pierced ears since I was 13, but it wasn't until I was 18 that I had them pierced eight times. My mother's reaction was to say I looked like a slut. She's used to it now. Although she's not so keen on my recent tongue piercing that I had craved for years! My dad was shocked when he found out about it, although he is well aware he can't do anything about it. He discovered it on a trip to visit my grandma in her nursing home and made me demonstrate for all the old folks. (Who weren't fazed in the slightest!)

Neither parent is keen on my tattoos. I have two, a bee on my hip and a small black star on my shoulder. I was going to stop there, but now I want another on my back. The excitement of getting a new tattoo is something special but I'm not sure why. They are very personal, with no two people's being the same. Mine have a special significance to me, especially the bee, which is the meaning of my name (honeybee). My little brother (aged 17) also now has a tattoo I discovered last time I was at home. My dad's reaction to that wasn't as extreme as his reaction to mine for some reason, even though it is twice as large and in a far more obvious place.

I don't know why I get tattoos. I know I think they're beautiful. They draw attention away from the actual flesh of me and to the tattoos themselves as art. Tattoos and piercings are common among my friends and people who are into the same sort of music as me. Maybe it's a way of identifying with others and fitting in. Most people I know have at least one piercing that isn't an earring (too normal) or navel (too trendy). Maybe I originally intended to annoy my parents and see how far I could push things. Except now I'm grown up and I still want more! When I got my tongue pierced this year it was a statement of freedom and individuality. I did it just after I stopped studying medicine to set me apart from the very normal people I had previously studied with. It also showed (or so I think) my intent not to go back to study something so conventional.

I know my mother doesn't really understand why I want to be scarring my body. She doesn't mind the piercings; she knows they will heal on their own. But tattoos are for life, or until laser surgery, anyway! I think she may feel that I'm scarring myself because I still don't like my body and that I'm trying to tell it who's boss. That's as maybe, but tattoos are much prettier than the other, self-inflicted scars I have. If you see them as scars, tattoos are a more socially acceptable way of hurting and scarring myself. I probably shouldn't do either. I call it bad anger management. I get angry and want to hurt people. So it makes sense to take myself away and hide and hurt myself instead.

Sometimes the anger is because I feel fat and ugly, that no one likes me and I hate myself. It often emerges when I have been out and felt ignored or left out. Somewhere in my brain this turns into the idea that no one ever likes me; how could they when I look so bad? And what's the point in living? I get into a completely panicked state and the suicidal thoughts scare me and make it worse. Sometimes all I need is a tiny scratch; at other times it takes many deeper cuts. I should say that I'm never actually trying to kill myself, just trying to stop myself wanting to!

So you might be surprised to know that in some ways I am kind of happy with both my body and myself now. I've learned how to use my body to work for me. I've been told I'm stunning and am never short of boyfriends; in fact I tend to go through them in large numbers. Just to prove I can.

If you saw me walking down the street you'd see someone expressing her personality through her appearance and exuding confidence in how she looks. Obviously wanting to be looked at. And I don't care whether people stare because they think I'm attractive, or because they can't believe anyone would go out looking like I do. It's all the same. I like to get a reaction and I'll admit that sometimes I dress to shock. I love to get disapproving looks from anyone, be it trendy kids, mothers or older people. I am a great fan of T-shirts with slogans on them, the more risqué the better as far as I'm concerned! My favourite at the moment has 'Blow up doll' across it, complete with an inflatable valve sewn on. It always gets comments! Maybe I'm just indulging my inner child and playing at dressing up, but anything goes as long as I find it appealing.

I don't think this apparent self-confidence is the whole story. Sometimes I use my clothes and make up to hide my body and myself. It's not me you're seeing, just an image of someone I wish I could be. There's always something else I could change or add to improve myself physically. Maybe then I'll be beautiful. Until then, I shall just have to settle for unique. I know which I'd prefer.

Sporty

Anna Maffioli

At primary school I stood out. The majority of other girls had long hair, were girlie, dressed in quite a feminine way and weren't exactly what I'd call the 'sporty type'. But I was singular: I had short hair, was strong, tall and more mature than the others and was very sporty. I wore trousers, shirts, sports clothing and had boys as my best friends. I was often mistaken for a lad. It didn't really upset me; I was me and the only one who knew me was me. I am a strong build like my father and, like my mother, I don't take any crap!

When I started my new school aged 10 I was hoping to make a fresh start. But on the very first day we were getting changed for PE and several girls were so convinced that I was a boy that they told me to leave the changing room. I handled it well, explaining patiently that I was a girl, and continued to get changed with small, embarrassed apologies from the girls around me. Unfortunately this experience slightly put me off PE as I didn't relish the prospect of going back into the changing room, but I was determined not to be discouraged as I loved the subject. It also wasn't exactly the best introduction to the people who would become my year, my class and my friends, but I was determined to stay as I was.

I went on through year seven, being taunted on and off by year eight and year nine pupils, many of them girls who thought there must be something wrong with me. They made out that I was a cross-dresser and shouted names like 'Trannie Annie' at me. When my mum found out she was outraged but, being a teacher, she knows what some kids are like. She believes that no one has the right to tease someone else, particularly when it becomes cruel. We agreed that she would phone school and as a result the name calling stopped for a while and I became happier. I spoke to some of the teachers and we discussed how much more mature I was than other girls. Mum also advised me not to give the abuse the attention that it was seeking. It was easy to keep a straight face when I was teased, but I still hurt inside.

I'm not sure if people assumed that I was gay because no one would say it to my face. I'm not gay, but do have ideas as to what attractive is. I can look at a girl and assume that lads find her attractive, and might even point one out to my male friends to see what they think.

It seemed to me that the boys accepted me better than the girls; I guess that I got on better with them because of the way I looked and because of my interest in sports and music. The girls only wanted 'normal' girls as their friends.

But I didn't want to become a boy. I was happy being myself, Anna, knowing that no one else was like me. I used to swear not to let it get to me; I would not become one of those people who was only interested in how people looked, rather than in their qualities.

I was always up for a laugh and although some of the boys' humour was sexually offensive, they were always an amusing crowd. At break and lunch the boys who I hung around with would be in our school's basketball court, which was where I always played basketball and football. I didn't know how to cope around girls because I worried that they all felt the same way about me. I didn't want to face any rejection so just stuck to what I was used to. I had a few friends who were boys who moved up to high school with me and I used to hang around with them. These days I still walk to school with my friend Hits, who lives around the corner from me. We used to tease each other in primary school and fell out frequently, but we have stuck together through thick and thin.

All the way through year seven, in order to survive, I toughened up and wouldn't take nothing from anyone who tried to put me down. I wouldn't back down from being me. I wouldn't and won't change for anyone. I continued to play basketball and even performed on guitar in front of a couple of hundred people, with Hits on sitar.

The taunting from the girls carried on as I moved into year eight. The year nine girls would make stupid jokes, like asking me out for their girlie friends and constantly telling me that I couldn't be a girl because of my hair and voice. I began to think up ways to get back at them. Eventually all the feelings I had bottled up came out and I would start to cry and often took my anger out on the wrong people. The people who suffered the most were my parents and friends.

Two years ago, at Christmas, I started going to karate classes with a male friend, Nagga, whom I have known for a very long time. I loved it because I would go along to the classes on Fridays and squeeze out all the anger that I had acquired over the week from people taunting me. I imagined that they were right there before me as I practised my techniques. It made me less aggressive towards my parents.

On the surface I became even harder and I began to retaliate. Since then I have noticed more and more that people have backed off and let me be. Gradually I have become my own person and have recently started to develop friendships with other girls; perhaps I was being prejudiced in writing them all off. I've started to find it easier to be with them and I now spend most of my time with girls. I enjoy their more sensible humour and the fact that they can laugh quite easily at themselves. The lads have started to annoy me; forever talking about girls in a rather disrespectful way and going on incessantly about wrestling and fights.

At the moment I have good friendships with two different girl groups. We laugh a lot, play around a lot and like pretty much the same lads, two in particular (not mentioning any names!) I jump from one friendship group to another but my real feelings of 'belonging' are with some of the girls in my 'band' (half of the year group). I can tell them things that are on my mind and they will help me; they have been supportive when I have been bullied or teased and I have helped them with their problems.

Every year at my school we have inter-form competitions. I usually play 'male' sports like football, but earlier this year I competed in the netball competition – a girl's sport – and really enjoyed it.

I realise that most boys at my school think that girls are rubbish at sports. When I was 10 I used to go to a basketball club that was held at the school that I want to attend next year. I was always the only girl and some instructors also believed that I was a boy and would talk to me as if I were one. I was better than a lot of the boys. Even now I am the only girl who does football in PE with about twenty-five lads. I've never really said this before but it's great! Some of them are attractive and are brilliant to watch. To be honest, it's good fun and I sometimes laugh at how seriously the lads take the games.

I recently decided to change my image, grow my hair longer and look slightly more feminine. Although I'm now being annoyed by my hair's untidiness and part of me wants to have it cut, having longer hair should make it easier to move up to my next school. All I know is that I'm the same person, and that people either like me for who I am, or not. People act like they seem to think that no matter what a person is like inside, it's only their looks that make them what they are and the sad thing is sometimes even I do this. I like the fact that there are no 'normal' people on this planet. Everyone is different and it's great.

I have very clear ideas about the direction that I want to go in. Mum and Dad have taught me to value education and that is what I do. One way I found to express myself is by writing. I love to write stories, songs, poems and scripts. My mum and dad have really encouraged me to get involved in this book because they and I know that I have something to offer to girls who don't conform to conventional thinking on what it is to be feminine.

Milestones

Lucy Parkin

Me and my mum are very similar in lots of ways. The old saying, 'If you want to see what a girl will be like when she's older then look at her mum.' is becoming scarily true! We sort of look the same: we've both got short hair and green eyes, but I'm about half an inch taller and half a size thinner. Mum's got cyclist's legs – she cycles everywhere – whereas mine are just regular legs. I walk with my feet turned in and my toes are short; some of my friends call them chipolatas. My mum is browner from more years in the sun and wears glasses and big earrings. I've got my nose pierced but she's only got her ears done.

Mum's not old. Even though she's 50, there's no oldness about her. She's into skater trainers and trousers and labels like Mambo and Quiksilver. She wears the clothes that teenagers would like to wear but can't because they're poor. She finds out about them from my friends. I sometimes borrow her clothes. She works in a Doc Martens seconds place where boots are £10–15 for us, so we've got about twenty pairs between Mum, her partner and me.

It's a bit like *Absolutely Fabulous* in our house – except I'm less boring than Saffie! Whether the subject is toxic shock syndrome or sex, sex and more sex, over a bottle – or three – of Chianti, you can always be sure that rudeness will be the presiding factor. Our kitchen table has witnessed some of the rudest, most outrageous conversations known to man. Perhaps I should say it has witnessed some of the rudest, most outrageous conversations known to 'woman'. I have these conversations with my mum, her partner – Belinda – and their friends. Odd though it might seem, my mum is the rudest, most liberated person I know. Just yesterday in a conversation with one of her friends I found out she has always been sex mad. I think that she likes to be seen as an eccentric, mad woman, revelling in unpredictable words and action.

Sitting around that table, I'm not a main participant in these conversations and sometimes I do cringe at the things Mum comes up with (just like Saffie!). Things that my own friends wouldn't dream of saying. She once decided to educate a male friend of mine on the joys of female ejaculation while we were all in the car. I don't think it needs to be said that the rest of us shut up fairly quickly and no one really knew how to pick up the conversation again! It's funny though that I don't really talk to my friends about sex all that much, and usually only in jest. I find it a little ironic that our supposedly promiscuous generation is actually much less comfortable with talking about sex than those who have more experience. I even have a problem writing about it.

Of course all this openness about bodies and sex used to embarrass me terribly. Being in a close female household it is not unusual for us to leave the bathroom door open or walk from the bath with no clothes on. This is fine until you reach the age of 14 and bring male friends home, who walk upstairs to the loo, only to be confronted by a naked 45-year-old woman! Saying that, though, as I've grown a little older and become a little more independent, I've stopped seeing Mum as an embarrassment and we've become really good friends. She gets on well with my friends, sometimes even better than I do.

Despite my mum's example I never realised that I had it in me to be so open about these subjects. I've become more liberated in the last couple of months since exams, travelling in Europe with a couple of friends. I actually instigated some discussions – tamer than at home, but still on the risqué side! It was the first time that I have talked openly about sex with friends and it took some guts to put my trust in them. It was a mutual feeling. We are all in sexual relationships and had left partners at home. Being in the same situation, coupled with free-flowing *vin de table* (at the English equivalent of 67 pence per litre!), meant we felt more comfortable with each other. We agreed not to tell others what we'd discussed, and I don't think that any of us has broken that pact as yet.

One of the reasons why I've been cagey is that most of my friends are straight and I'm going out with a girl. I've been with Tessa for a year and a half, since sixth form. I've had a couple of semi-short relationships with boys but now I'm in love. I don't see my sexuality as the biggest part of my life; it doesn't really define who I am as a person. I don't particularly look like a lesbian, whatever a lesbian is supposed to look like. I get on really well with Tessa's family. I don't know who they were expecting to walk in – someone in leathers and chains – but I think they were glad that I seemed normal. Tessa is slightly more feminine than I am; she wears skirts and I don't that often. Neither of us has an image relating to our sexuality; we're just ourselves.

I was always brought up to think that I'm beautiful and that anyway it's infinitely more important what sort of person you are. I am who I am and that's OK. When I was about 11 or 12 I had a bad year when I felt awful about my body. I thought I was too fat and everyone called me the fat swot. I was always quite fat but never really thought about it. I was living with my dad around that time and he worshipped the ground I walked on. He always saw me as a little girl and found it hard to accept that I was becoming a young woman. Later on, when I moved to live with my mum again, we did a de-tox fat-free thing to support Delinda, who had developed allergies to dairy products. We stopped eating cheese, butter and chocolate for nine months. In the first six months I lost quite a lot of weight and as a result felt a lot more confident about my body.

One outcome of the openness and liberation at home is that I have become happy with my body and with myself. As well as being outrageous it is a very supportive environment where anyone can turn up (and they do) and have their spirits boosted. I have learned to find the positives in people and allow them to find the positives in me. Of course I have the same angst as any teenager about whether my bum looks big or whether my stomach is flat enough, but I don't let this override the fact that I am happy with who I am on the inside. I believe that I am a good person (with flaws, I admit), but in essence someone who is friendly, loyal and fun to be around. I see my physicality more as a vehicle for the expression of my soul than as a representation of the real me, which is in my head. Perhaps I sound as though my body is not important to me in its own right; it is but not as important as my mind. I am a great believer in the fusion between body and soul. For one to be healthy and function effectively the other must also.

I know all too well about both malfunctioning. I have had friends with fairly serious body-image problems, expressed in a variety of ways, such as anorexia and self-harm. I don't believe though that these are triggered by the body; they are more of a physical expression of the soul's discontent and a cry for help. We discuss things like this around our table, too, which could be why I value our discussions so much. Diametric opposites of fun and seriousness, but with the overriding knowledge that anything goes. There are no boundaries of what we talk about so perhaps I was wrong when I said that rudeness is the prevailing factor. Maybe openness is, but openness breeds rudeness on many occasions. We have made some pretty big decisions there, too, like the one we made last year to get tattoos for our birthdays.

It was my mum's 50th birthday and my 18th two days later. We'd decided years ago that we would buy each other something permanent for the milestones in both our lives. My mum got a butterfly on her arm, while my tattoo is a small green and yellow lizard on my shoulder, called Rupert. It means a lot to me. It's a representation of my mum's love but also a representation of her constancy, and my own. It will always be there; no matter what else happens in my life Rupert will be on my shoulder ready to scamper down my back. I will always have a reminder of who I am and where I have been. I don't want to forget and yet I want to change, grow and evolve. Rupert is a reminder of that; wherever I am, I am still me in essence, inside and out.

Scratch

Esther Linton

My skin gets irritated when I'm anxious about something. It's like it's about to erupt, so I start to scratch and then the soreness begins. Yep – I've got eczema.

Nowadays you can hardly tell I've got it and most of the time it's more of a sensation that I can feel, rather than anything other people can see, but when I was younger I was very aware of it. My eczema is usually brought on by stress or something in the air and the best way to cure it is to take away whatever is aggravating it in the first place. The stress can be caused by an argument, an emotion I'm feeling, or if someone else is going through something that I don't know how to deal with. Sometimes when I'm in a group and I want to say something but don't feel articulate enough to express myself, I'll start scratching. It's a subconscious thing, I'll just scratch.

Sheets can also make me itch if they're not cotton or if they've been washed in biological powder. I used to take my own sheets and pillow case when I stayed over with friends, otherwise I'd find bloodspots because I'd be lying in bed scratching away at night-time. When I slept with my boyfriend Mark he'd always be telling me to stop scratching and my sister (who I shared bunk beds with) used to say it sounded like bees buzzing round the room. She'd shout 'Stop scratching!' but I didn't always know I was doing it because most times I'd be asleep. If I was awake I'd be desperately trying to think about something else, to take my mind off it. I've tried wearing cotton gloves to stop myself from scratching but I always want to pull them off.

Depending on how severe my eczema attack is, there are three options to treat it, all involving loading cream onto my skin. The first level, if it's a mild attack, is a moisturiser; the next is an ointment; and the last is a steroid cream. I've always tried to avoid taking any tablets. I have to put the creams on at least twice a day, in the morning and at night-time. My mum used to help me with my back but I always wanted to do it myself; I wasn't very good at asking for help and it had to be done firmly and thoroughly. The ointment feels like sticky glue that's plastered on you. I've always loved hugging people but when my skin was bad I wouldn't want to go near anyone. I'd keep my arms and legs apart so that everything could breathe.

My skin used to feel really dirty, covered in this sticky thick ointment, with the fishy smell of the eczema when it was bad. The cream would get stuck to my clothes, and it felt like fibreglass over all my body. Sticky and awkward. One of my teachers had it and the kids used to say 'Ugh, she smells of fish.' No one ever said anything to me like that; my friends were kind-hearted.

Having eczema made me shy and insecure when I was at school because I wanted to hide, to avoid too much attention. I felt that I was always noticed as the one with eczema, while other people would be identified by their hair colour, their height or other characteristics. People did respect me though because I always stood my ground in my own little way and no one ever called me names. But when I was 17 or 18 and at college it got worse; partly due to the pressures of growing up and partly because I was missing my friends from school. I was also upset because they were going to university and I wasn't; I felt a bit of a failure.

In the past my eczema sometimes prevented me from going out, mainly because it was so uncomfortable but also because of how it looked, especially if it came up on my face. I would really hate it when I wanted to look sexy to go out clubbing. I've got a fantastic figure, which I love to show off, but it was spoilt by the way my skin looked. I ended up wearing clothes that would completely cover my arms, legs and back, so then I felt hot and itchy. This limited my choice of outfits, especially because I had to wear material that wouldn't irritate my skin. Mostly I chose cotton, but I would have preferred something clingy and sexy like Lycra. Having said that, I was lucky: I never had any problem pulling men!

When I first started having sex I felt insecure; embarrassed and unsure about my body, wondering if I was normal. I didn't really feel sexy because I was always focusing on what I could improve on and it always came down to my skin, my bloody eczema. It was difficult if I got hot or, worse still, if my lover got sweaty because I was allergic to sweat. His stubble and aftershave could also affect my eczema and it would always flare up just when I didn't want it to, stopping me from getting close. Sexually it was a big issue for me and I'd want to hide myself if I got out of bed to go to the toilet.

I hated wearing a swimming costume because it exposed so much of my skin and the eczema was on the back of my knees, the inside of my elbows and on my back. Friends would persuade me to go swimming because I loved it once I was in the water but I developed a bit of a complex about people staring at me. To overcome it, I would either jump in really quickly or just focus on the friends I was with. The chlorine didn't help as it made my skin flare up. Baths were bad, too, so I put lots of medicated oil in the water but this made me feel like I had cling film all over my body. Without oil my skin would itch so much I'd rub it like mad with a towel when I was drying myself, making it really sore, as if I'd taken a layer of skin off. Sometimes the itchiness was so bad I'd scratch myself with a soft hair brush.

It was worse in the summer when I was hot. There were times when I went swimming in a hot country and looked at all the beautiful skin around and felt jealous. It's crazy really because I know I've got a good body and people get jealous of my figure, but it never crosses their minds that I might be jealous of their skin. Going on holiday I wanted to wear shorts and short sleeves but was always trying to find lightweight clothes that could completely cover me up so that other people wouldn't see my skin. I was constantly aware of what they might think of me, particularly guys.

Environment and different conditions – such as dust, dirt, humidity and even soap powder – in other countries can make a huge difference. The worst time I ever had with my eczema was when I was travelling in Asia. I was away for about five months, travelling through Thailand, Cambodia, Burma and Bali, and was planning to carry on around the world but had to cut my holiday short as my skin became so bad. It was because of a build-up of a number of things: the hot sticky air meant that my skin felt it couldn't breathe, I ran out of non-bio washing powder, I probably wasn't drinking enough water and we were constantly on the move, with new dust, new dirt all the time. I was starting to feel run-down and tired and this was having a knock-on effect on my skin. I'd had such a great time up until that point but by now I had eczema from head to toe and it had become infected. Once it starts to get out of control it's very hard to get it to heal again, so you really have to nip it in the bud. My eyelids became pussy and would get stuck together; I was so scared, waking up and not being able to open one of my eyes. It was torture. The doctor tried to help, prescribing me antibiotics and antihistamines and different creams, but nothing worked. It just wouldn't heal in the heat, so I would lie in an air-conditioned bedroom feeling hopeless. When I went out the local Balinese people would look at me with a shocked expression and ask what had happened. My skin was red raw. I just wanted to rip it off and was scratching like mad. I felt disgusting and eventually I had to fly home.

There are some funny ideas about eczema; that you might catch it, like it's the lurgy. I think people thought I was a bit dirty because I felt uncomfortable in my skin and I just wanted to hide away from them. When I was about 8 years old one girl told me not to sit on her bed in case she 'caught that stuff' on me. When it's really bad you feel out of the norm, ugly, like you don't fit in. It was such a relief when I met other sufferers and we talked about our experiences with it; realising that I was not alone.

I am so glad that I've recently more or less conquered my eczema. I did a self-development course about a year ago, which built up my confidence. Since then I've made lots of changes: got rid of stresses in my life, looked after myself, changed my job and moved away from home. My last holiday in Greece was brilliant because I could wear anything and I got a tan, which helped to cover up the scars. Now I can sweat with no problem and I feel sexy again!

Confidence

Gemma Wilkins

I was always 'the little fat kid' as a child. I grew up with my mother, an unemployed single parent, and my brother, as irritating a sibling as I could wish for. We didn't have a lot of money for fancy, expensive clothes. It didn't matter; being of a stout build I couldn't wear tight tops and short skirts without looking like a cream slice after someone bites into it! I was happy with shapeless T-shirts and baggy trousers. This was all I wore until I was 13. I just didn't care. I was more concerned with fitting in and wanted to be accepted by people as a person, not the fat kid.

Unfortunately I spent the first eight years of my education in a school system dominated by those who felt that your clothes defined you. Those who could squeeze themselves into the least amount of cloth possible (short skirts, tight trousers, bikinis) were the most powerful in our primitive hierarchy. Those who, like me, found buying clothes that fitted a task most closely related to looking for a needle in a haystack were on the periphery of social gatherings. We were left off party lists and found sitting alone at school discos. The majority were those who, by virtual starvation, could just about jam themselves into the right clothes, the latest craze, and thus maintain a position that was acceptable to the masses. Forget about finding an individual style. Back then, even more than today, we were overlooked in magazines and on TV; it was in the days before Lisa Riley. With a choice between unaffordable clothes that didn't fit or shapeless one-size-fits-all (if you're an elephant) cast-offs, I didn't really stand a chance.

And it wasn't just clothes I got wrong. I didn't like the right music. In a desperate attempt to be accepted, having had no luck with my looks, I feigned a devotion to Take That. Only I could have chosen them at the very peak of their unpopular phase. But how was I to know? I wasn't bothered by the music charts; I didn't care which identical cover of a previously good song had got to number 1. It wasn't that I didn't like music; I just hadn't found the type that I really loved. At that stage in my life I was living in a kind of limbo, wondering how to behave.

I didn't understand a lot of things about being an individual until I started a new school at the age of 14. By this time my mum had remarried and we had more money, but habit and security kept me in the same clothes. I was bullied in my last school and expected it to happen again. I figured if I was going to be bullied, I might as well be bullied in the clothes I was used to!

Upon arrival at my new school I set about learning my way around and trying to find an ally; something I usually failed miserably at. I found myself among the less despised of the outcasts, in a situation that was far removed from being popular but couldn't be deemed being a loner. In short I became average. I managed to survive for a while; staying afloat and treading water. Then we got the note from the teachers: we were going to have a non-uniform day.

Time to panic. I returned to my huge T-shirt (the T standing for tent) and wandered meekly into school. I was prepared for sniggering and filthy looks, though these were in shorter supply than before. What I wasn't prepared for was my friends, the freaks. They were wearing clothes I could afford and that actually looked acceptable. They told me where to find them and I went shopping, buying clothes and mixing them into a unique style all my own. I discovered denim, and Lycra/cotton mixes. I learned that I didn't have to wear tops down to my knees, but could look presentable in shorter clothes. Not armpit short, but waist short or just-above-knee short! It was more the style than the actual clothes themselves.

It wasn't so much that these clothes defined me, it was more that they were me. Wearing them felt as natural as breathing. They went with the music my friends listened to, which happened to be the music I'd been searching for. I had discovered heavy metal, grunge and rock music. The idea of wearing anything bearing the lyric Seek and Destroy shocked my mother but really appealed to me. I finally managed to get away from hand-knitted jumpers and into the darker side of music. My friends taught me not to care what other people thought, just to do what I was comfortable with. That was when I found out who I really was.

It was so much easier after that. Having people around who weren't ashamed to be seen talking to me boosted my confidence, and having friends to guide me helped no end! New school – new start. About six people at my new school had known me at my old school but, not out of any particular kindness to me, more to further their own social status, they forgot they'd ever met me. That suited me fine.

At first it was great just to be myself and not have to try and live up to anything. But, as I learned more and more about who I was, I found myself doing more and more outrageous things. I went through phases, experimented. At first it was just less baggy shirts and nicer trousers. Then came skirts and dresses. Then I reverted to trousers when I went through my tomboy phase. I donned blue overalls and took a Saturday job as a car mechanic. I began experimenting with eyeliner, finding some interesting things to do with it and started wearing clothes that would make Sid Vicious blush!

Finally I found an image that fitted me and that I was comfortable with, settling into a happier life, a life in which I was accepted by others simply because I had accepted myself. Maybe it was because we had grown up and discovered that people were different. Maybe it was just me that grew up, realising I didn't have to be a clone to function properly in society. I was also surprised to find that I wasn't really as fat as I thought I was. I was just a bit bigger than average (size 16–18). I still couldn't escape the cream slice look if I wore short tops, but I just avoided those clothes.

Now when I meet new people, they don't believe me when I say how unpopular and unconfident I used to be. I don't have any photographs from that period in my life, simply because we couldn't afford a camera. I smile as I tell them and laugh at their disbelief! And it works in reverse as well. People I went to school with can't believe it's the same me. Like I said, gone are the baggy T-shirts. Now I'm found in bright and colourful clothes that make me stand out from my friends, who find comfort in black and black!

Sometimes I go the opposite way. I dress myself in the blackest clothes I can find, draw strange symbols (pentagons, spiders, cobwebs, random patterns) on my face and go out with my friends, looking for the ridicule I once feared. I still have to laugh every time we do this. We go out in force, and watch with fascination as the people that we were always scared of cross the road when they see us coming. That's what I call justice!

My image isn't that important to me now. It suits me, but I seem to have become a product of what I wear. By that I mean that other people look at me and know things about me that I didn't tell them. Not life-changing, just little character traits. It's true that people do judge on appearances, which is all well and good if you don't look one thing and act another. I don't agree with this but I try and limit the damage by reflecting my personality in my clothes as much as possible.

I've just started university, and the people I've met there judge me by my clothes, but not necessarily in a horrible way. One girl, after talking to me for five minutes, and having met me just two hours ago, suddenly turned my purse over, smiling in triumph when she found a turtle pin-badge stuck to the front. 'I knew you'd have something on there,' she said. Another woman on my course cornered me after a couple of weeks and told me where I could get some leather trousers quite cheaply. This made me laugh; how she had worked out I wear them I don't know. All I'd worn up to that point was jeans (denim not leather) and what my friends refer to as 'Gemma tops', which range from plain white to black with silver cobwebs, red to torn and tie-dyed, sparkly to black and almost obscene!

I still don't like to be judged too much by my clothes. Every now and then I do something no one will expect. I wait until people think they have got me worked out and then I'll go to a seminar in fishnet stockings and black lipstick. This is a style I adopted from one of my biggest vices: The Rocky Horror Picture Show. People's preconceived ideas about me are still overturned the first time they find out about this obsession!

If you're interested in how far my image has shifted, I'll tell you a bit more about how I look now. I'm much more confident. I have blood-red hair at the moment, and two tattoos; a clover in a horseshoe on my ankle and a bear on my hip. Even though I wasn't born until the 1980s I have to confess I am a product of the 1970s, pure and simple. Punk rock and glitter all the way, baby!

So, here I am. Happy with the way I look, and just out for a laugh like everyone else. If I'd realised so many years ago that it wasn't what I wore that made people shun me, but rather my own self-dislike, things could have been different. If I can't like myself, how can I expect anyone else to? If someone had told me that, just once in passing, I like to think I'd have been accepted sooner. Then again, being accepted earlier might have made me become someone else, and I like who I am now. Besides, it was because of my image that I didn't have the confidence to like myself, and my image was the result of my self-hating lack of confidence. Catch 22!

Now I'm annoyed that I spent all those years trying to be something I wasn't, just to fit in. I wouldn't have minded so much if it had worked, but I was still outcast. It was only after I found my own style (and me) that I was accepted, because I had the confidence to be different.

Changing

Susie Nathan

Picture the scene. The communal changing room. Rows of benches, lockers and hooks, three-quarters of a metre apart. The musty smell of sweaty trainers mixed with steam from the showers. And no privacy! Twenty-five girls crammed together, trying desperately to keep their bodies covered while changing into A-line skirts and T-shirts. Everyone conspicuously looking to seek comparisons with their classmates, to check that their bodies are developing correctly.

First off is the jumper, then the shoes. You sit on a bench and try to take off your thick black tights. The girl next to you is struggling to undo her tightly knotted shoelaces and her head is level with your legs. You know your legs resemble milk bottles (it's been so long since summer) and you've got stretch marks running along the inside of your thighs. If she sees them she'll tell her friend who's mates with the boy you fancy and your chances with him will be ruined. So you unroll the waistband of your skirt to lengthen it, stand up, rip off your tights and pull on a pair of cycling shorts faster than you can blink. That's obstacle number one over with; now for number two. You have to get your T-shirt on without revealing the large sling-shot-style bra your mum makes you wear. Pull the T-shirt over your head and unbutton the shirt whilst simultaneously tugging the T-shirt over your chest. You know that someone's seen the bra, you just weren't quick enough. What are people going to think?! Will the boy you fancy hear that you're wearing a granny-style bra? You take a quick look around you at all the other girls trying to hide away with similarly bizarre methods of undressing and dressing and wonder if you'll always be so embarrassed about your body.

Is everyone else this paranoid? Surely not those popular girls in the corner, semi-naked and comparing their sexy bra & knicker sets. How could they hate their bodies yet stand there showing them off? Look at them: perfect small breasts, perfect slim waists, perfect bottoms and perfect thighs. Their skin tanned and pimple free and not a stretch mark in sight. They go on holiday four times a year, either to their parents' villas in the Algarve or some other sunny destination, so they have a continuous tan all year round. You can almost see expensive lotions and potions oozing from their skin.

These were the kind of girls that everyone at my school envied. They were the popular girls who only hung out with the popular boys who were, as expected, well groomed and drop-dead gorgeous. Girls like me could only dream about getting close to these Adonises-in-training. We could only stand on the sidelines and watch the beautiful people dating, dumping and moving on, with no hope of ever joining their select group. All we wanted was to look as good as these girls.

I was an early developer. At primary school I was the second girl in my year to get boobs. I was mortified. The boys were typical boys, poking and prodding and calling me names. The girls were harder to handle though. Most were curious, wondering if my boobs hurt and how they made me feel, and telling me how grown up and mature they made me look. But there was also a group who made my life hell. They teased me relentlessly, pinging my straps so hard my back was red raw. The teachers were unsupportive; they didn't even seem to notice what was happening in the classroom, right in front of their eyes. I dreaded taking off my jumper because my bra would show and, even on the hottest days, it remained on.

When I started secondary school I found that although my boobs were bigger than many others, I wasn't the only one who'd started early. This left me feeling a little better but I still had insecurities. Along with my boobs came another problem, namely puppy fat. Suddenly I was no longer a lithe, athletic kid but a chubby teenager with boobs and a complex. Before this I'd been very good at gymnastics, with walking the beam being my forte. However, I soon lost my sense of balance and gave up on my dream of entering competitions and eventually on gymnastics altogether. Sometimes I felt that the only reason I looked good was because of my cleavage, so I'd flaunt it a little more. I would wear tight clothes that showed off my cleavage with baggy shirts and cardigans over the top to hide the flab. But I was never truly happy with myself. I wanted so much to be thin and to wear the fantastic clothes that

I saw in the magazines and shops, or at least borrow my friends' stuff.

By 14, being so well-endowed did have some advantages. With the right clothes, a little make-up, some guts and an attitude, I could pass for much older. I was able to buy cigarettes, alcohol and could easily get into clubs. But that led to other issues and problems. Looking 18 and being well-endowed, although more than a little chubby, meant men noticed me more than boys of my own age did. Having had little self-confidence since primary school, I was susceptible to flattery and charm and could have found myself in a lot of trouble. But luckily I had a sensible head on my shoulders and was able to extract myself from situations before they went too far or became nasty. Others, however, were not always so fortunate.

Me and my five closest friends were never invited to the parties that the popular kids threw every week. Instead we found our own entertainment. We would dress up, put on our make-up, lie to our parents, meet at a local tube station and go somewhere local or head up to London's West End. We weren't old enough to get into pubs or clubs, but we would hang out and try to meet people. Or should I say boys and men! You might say we were tarts, and you would be right; you might also say we were slags, but there you would be wrong. We just wanted male attention.

We would go to the cinema, arrive early and hang about trying to find some good-looking guys. Then we'd position ourselves in their sight and try to attract their attention. We'd be loud and funny and try to make it look like we were having the most fun ever. Eventually we would catch some poor guys and latch onto them for the night. It was a successful night if one or more of us got a snog and telephone numbers. Sometimes we would see the guys again. Sometimes not. As we got older, the snogs led onto other things and some of my friends went a little further than they should have.

My friend Lily was a girl with very little self-confidence. She wasn't bad-looking, but was slightly out of proportion and looked a little top-heavy. As we got older she became boy-crazy. On our Saturday nights out she'd be the most outrageous flirt and always got a couple of numbers. But she'd take it further and sometimes disappear for a couple of hours with a guy. She'd tell us all about it after and sometimes I wish she hadn't. At the age of 14 Lily lost her virginity to a boy she barely knew in the toilets of our local McDonalds and she carried on with her mad exploits until we left school.

Being friends with Lily meant that we were all tarred with the same brush and were sometimes approached by the boys at school, who thought that we would be willing to perform sexual favours in return for a couple of cigarettes. Last time I spoke with her we were reminiscing about our school days. She told me how she regretted losing her virginity in such an impersonal way, and wished that she'd waited for someone she really cared about. I told her that even though I had waited until I was of age, and for someone I had feelings for, I still felt that I had been too young and immature for sex and wished I had waited longer till I'd been more sure of my own identity.

I've realised that teenagers are subject to lots of influences and peer pressure, which can make us preoccupied with our image and our social status. A dissatisfied teenager can spend years trying to mould themselves into something they aren't, until they realise they were happier before they started. As we become adults, we have to come to terms with our own identity and understand that we have to create our own niche in the world, tailor-made to suit us. However, when you're a teenager, it's often the little things (or the things that are too big!) that seem to matter.

Rules

Fatima Patel

The image that my family, cousins, and aunts strive to achieve can be summed up by these three words; Sophistication, Elegance and Class. SEC for short. It was me that came up with SEC and it's a sort of standing joke in my family. The only way to be successful at SEC is to wear clothes that cost a fortune, such as Gucci and Chanel, which means that I live in fear of dropping food down my front.

Dressing according to this code does, however, give me a bit more leeway than most girls I know who are restricted to traditional Muslim-Asian clothing. My family doesn't expect me to dress in that way, which is quite a liberated way of thinking for Muslim-Asians. I'm allowed to wear trousers or long skirts down to my ankles and tops that come at least to the waist, rather than a shalwar kameez (a loose fitting long dress). The only condition is that I respect my religion and do not expose any body parts except for my hands, feet and hair. When the women in my family wear make-up, we don't apply it excessively so that it looks garish, but to be honest I've stopped using it altogether unless it's a special occasion.

At school I knew a few Asian girls who didn't want to wear the traditional clothes. As soon as they got to school each morning they would take off their headscarves and shalwar kameez and change into a miniskirt and tight top. I realised when I was 16 that my school friends (many of whom were Asian) were spending more time in the school toilets than in our form room. Being naturally curious, I wanted to know what all the fuss was about. They were putting on each others' make-up and sharing tips on clothes and I discovered these rules:

1. Wear clothes that show off your body to the best possible advantage – the tighter the better.
2. Pack on as much make-up as possible, leaving no area of skin uncovered.
3. Wear the biggest heels you can find. This tends to become an obsessive competition after a while, involving buying shoes every week just to outgrow the girl after you in the register.

So did I try all of the above? I did but tight clothes just made me look anorexic, make-up made me come up in spots, and heels gave me backache. I think I lasted all of a week before I gave up. The feeling that I was becoming another one of those faceless thousands of 16-year-olds and losing my own identity became just that little bit too much.

I've never really bothered much with heels. Being 5 foot 7 put me above other girls anyway, let alone adding a 3-inch heel to it. I was once told that if you see a tall Asian girl, look down at her shoes to see how high her heels are. So does being tall put me in a minority?

Luckily not in my family. Among my relatives I'm considered to be of average height.

Many Asian families do not allow girls to cut their hair, believing it makes them less respectable within the community. Because of this some girls go to extreme measures to have their hair cut. One incident I've heard about involved a girl who wasn't allowed to have her hair cut so deliberately burnt it to the length she wanted. Another girl smeared chewing gum down her hair and left it to dry so it then had to be cut.

I chose a simpler course of action: I simply walked into the hairdressers and asked for a cut. My family has no qualms about cutting your hair if it makes you feel good about yourself and if you obey the religious rule that a female does not resemble a male. Personally I think medium-length hair gives a girl a sophisticated, feminine look and it is really helpful when you want to shield your face during embarrassing moments (like when your great aunt decides to pinch your cheek in greeting in a room full of people). My hair also gave me huge problems when it came to spots, and yes, I got them too. I had a clear complexion until I hit 14 but then those spots came out with a vengeance. I found that I continually pulled my hair forward to cover my face, but this just led to more spots.

Clear, fair skin seems to be a real bonus in the Asian community. I myself am not really fair but I'm not considered to be dark either; I'm somewhere in between. It's hard to explain why having light skin is so important, because I don't fully understand it myself. If you ask an Asian person to describe their ideal partner, fair always turns up on the two-page list. This I feel is not always just the case with the Asian community, but also with white people in the west. Cinderella was fair and beautiful, as well as Sleeping Beauty, and the name Snow White just says it all. So why do we obsess about skin colour? I think there are a number of reasons but white seems to symbolise purity and goodness. Notice how if you're fair you can get away with wearing all those feminine pastel colours but if you're dark you wear colours such as red, which is considered to be the colour of the flirt, the secret devil inside of you.

Another reason I feel that fair skin is favoured is that many native Indians are dark skinned. The lighter skin tone seems to come from people migrating from places of Arab origin. Being able to boast that your daughter-in-law is fair immediately has the neon sign 'ARAB ancestors' flashing in a person's head. Our family has no way of knowing exactly where we are descended from. Some say Iran, others say Persia, but that was centuries ago and since then we have settled mainly in India and Mauritius.

My mum and her family are quite liberal but we don't live with my dad any more. He was very strict. Mum's attitude is to hold on to your culture, keep the religion, get your education, live your life and enjoy yourself. By not putting too tight a control over us children it's meant that we respect our family and, as Nan says, it's a mutual respect thing.

Many girls revolt against family rules so my advice to parents is not to lay down laws and expect no questions. That just leads to arguments, screaming matches, doors being slammed around the house and the silent treatment for the rest of the week. I believe that parents need to be understanding at a time when their daughters are coming to an age where they are developing their own identity. We all need to accept who we are and how God intended us to be, rather than how society expects us to be. If you are not confident about yourself, most people will not take you seriously. You need to love yourself and know that others love you just the way you are. Those that really count won't judge you for the way you look, but for the person you are on the inside.

Boobs

Tasmin Smith

I first noticed my breasts starting to grow when I was about 13 and I can remember the day when I looked at myself in a tight top and could see their shape and felt proud. They were a double A, the same size as my friend Jennifer's. Then they started to grow and they grew and grew and now they're much bigger than hers. I'm a 34C/D and my breasts are among the biggest in my year.

In my gang we're forever examining our shape and size and proportions, always comparing ourselves to each other and to the rest of the girls in our year. For my height – I'm 5 foot 6 – I think my boobs are too big. My legs and arms are skinnier than the rest of my body, which makes my boobs and stomach seem even bigger. I've got quite big lips, too. I used to get bullied when I was younger and called rubber lips. Now older guys say they like them.

It takes me ages to get dressed to go out because I think I look awful in everything I wear. It's the same every time: I'm getting changed with my friends and I'm saying I look horrible but they're saying I look really skinny and really nice. I know Jackie means well but in a way I don't really believe her. She's saying it to get me to hurry up – well, I do take about two hours to get ready! Jackie and Jennifer say I'm really lucky because I've got quite a big cleavage and I can wear low tops but I feel frumpy, matronly, round, like an old woman, not light and girlish. My breasts weigh me down and make me lean forward and I've got round shoulders, too, with shoulder blades that stick out. Until recently I thought I looked like a hunchback!

I wear tight tops because I think they look more flattering than baggy ones. Sometimes I'll go out without a bra on, like if I'm wearing a sideways top with a shoulder down diagonal. The top holds my breasts in place, compact and round. I don't like anything that flattens them because then they spread out and look bigger.

I wear padded bras for the shape and because I don't like my nipples; the tips are small and don't stick out much. When they're not erect they sort of disappear. I thought I was really abnormal but seeing my friends Jackie's and Natalie's nipples made me feel better, theirs are similar to mine. Getting one of my nipples pierced has helped a lot because it keeps the nipple sticking out.

I had my nipple ring put in at the end of June. When I had it done it was really painful, the worst pain I've ever experienced in my life, much worse than my tattoo. I couldn't look; it felt like a spike was going into it. Before I had it done I spent a lot of time worrying that the nipple wouldn't be erect enough to be pierced so I checked that they would freeze it first. I asked my friend Christine about it as she'd already had hers done and she said it would be OK. To be doubly sure I made my friend Natalie go first. She's got the same type of nipples as mine and she was worried, too. It didn't hurt her as much; she just scrunched up her face.

I wanted the piercing in my nipple because I thought it would be something different and would look nice and my boyfriend at the time was quite keen on the idea. Plus my mum was insistent that I didn't have any piercings done on my face. I wasn't expecting it to help keep my nipple sticking out – that was just an added bonus.

I didn't let my boyfriend see my breasts even when we were having sex. I kept my bra on so that he couldn't see or touch my nipples in case they weren't erect. Jackie and Jennifer don't let theirs see their breasts either because they think theirs are too small, and Jodie has got the same type of nipples as mine. Boys think I'll get turned on by my breasts but I don't have very sensitive nipples, and so I'm not really interested in having them touched. My boyfriend kept trying and would feel them through the material because he really liked them. The one and only time I took my bra off while having sex I made sure the light was switched off first.

It's always my boobs, rather than anything else about me, that attract attention. Boys make comments like 'you've got big tits' and they mean it as a compliment but I'd rather get noticed for my looks or my personality.

Recently we found out that the boys in our year at school had been writing lists of who was good-looking and who was ugly. Nothing about personality – but then no surprise there! One list had all the girls in order of looks from the fittest to the ugliest. Another one listed the girls who would make up 'The Perfect Girl' in our school; I was on there for my boobs and hair, Jackie was included for her face, and another girl for her legs. They also had an 'Ugly Wanks' list and I discovered that I was on that, too. I couldn't believe it, especially as I had been out with quite of few of those boys, so I spoke to one of them, who said it was only a joke. I was really upset. I didn't show that I cared but I don't understand how they can be so hurtful.

Boys expect more from girls looks-wise. We're more interested in personality and in someone who can hold a conversation so we often end up going for slightly older guys because they're more mature.

I suppose I'm pretty self-conscious about my breasts because I notice everything; not just the size and the nipple shape but now also the nipple piercing itself, which is a ring with a ball. On holiday I wore a bikini, that wasn't padded so the ball on the nipple ring showed and it made me look like I had a second nipple on that breast. I became quite relaxed on holiday so I took my bikini top off when I was snogging with an Italian boy I met there. We were always kissing at night-time at the club on the beach and it was cold enough for my nipples to become erect. It was a holiday romance and I really fancied him but he wasn't that nice and slept around.

I lost my virginity last November when I was fifteen, but haven't had sex with anyone else since. I think that my big boobs make it look like I'm easy, which isn't at all true, but boys seem to think so. Some of the boys in the list-writing group said all I was good for was a good fuck. I also heard that from one of my exes; maybe they said it because I snogged loads of blokes at parties last summer. The fact that I just get noticed for my breasts makes me feel like a bit of a bimbo; like I'm not very intelligent and only into sex. I don't want to promote this idea so I tend to hold back from having sex but when I explain this to boys that I'm with they don't really understand. Quite a lot of boys fancy me, the breasts and lips being the main attraction. It's flattering but, as I said, I'd prefer it if they liked me for my face.

Tall

Jackie Harris

I think I'm average build but my friends say I'm slim: I'm a size 8. I've got mid-length dark brown hair with highlights, hazel eyes and a Madonna lip stud. I'm quite happy with my looks really, except that my breasts are a bit on the small side – 32B (just!) – and they're not in proportion to my hips, which are bigger. And the fact that my feet are big bugs me quite a lot. But the thing about my appearance that affects me the most is being tall.

At 5 foot 8 I stand out among my friends, attracting attention when I would rather blend into the crowd. People say it's good to be tall – like a model – and some girls say 'I wish I was taller, it makes you look slimmer.' Girls always say tall is attractive, but I've never really seen anyone who looks good because they're tall; they just look lanky and out of place. Being slim too I feel like a lanky beanpole.

I've also got really long legs, so all the trousers that fit length-wise are size 14 and much too big for me. There's a good range at Top Shop called Tall but generally it's so difficult to get trousers for long legs that I haven't got many pairs and my friends all dread shopping for trousers with me. I've got long arms too and I end up buying tops with three-quarter length sleeves that look like T-shirts on me. I've recently changed my style from a more classy image – jeans, boots, little cardi and tight tops – to a surf/skater look which makes me look shorter because the bagginess adds to my width.

I'm not keen on the fact that I stick out, especially when I'm standing with girls and a lot of my friends are shorter than me so I end up leaning over to talk to them. I've recently become friends with Jennifer, who at 5 foot 11 is even taller than me. It's great walking around town with her and when we went out last Friday night all the blokes couldn't believe how tall *she* was. Sometimes I like the fact that I get noticed and attract attention from men because of my height; I only recently realised that this is happening. At other times it holds me back because I feel self-conscious. Take last night, for example.

I went along to the karaoke night, a weekly event at Cases, a bar in Hastings town centre. I was really excited because it was the August Bank Holiday and packed. We'd gathered together with a group of people; some were friends of mine, some were a new, slightly older bunch. I was sinking the Smirnoff Ices, topped up with vodka from a bottle we'd snuck in (I was having to economise, having spent £25 on Friday night). We were sitting around talking about a bloke Tasmin was hoping to see. Towards the end of the evening all the girls in our group decided they were going to go on stage and do Atomic Kitten's 'Whole Again'.

I refused to go on because all the other girls were a lot shorter than me and I would have to stoop or otherwise stick out. I would definitely have to bend down to reach the microphone. Everyone was encouraging me to go up and sing, and I really did want to join in, but I just couldn't face it. I'd sung at a karaoke before, with a group of people at a christening party and had a photo taken. When I looked at it afterwards I could see that I was stooping.

I'd had a few drinks and was tipsy like everyone else when we were due to go and sing so you'd have expected a boozy courage to have helped me, but it still bothered me that I stood out, and even having a few drinks inside me wasn't enough to give me the confidence. Being tall is such a big thing for me. Jennifer didn't want to go up either and everyone thought we were really boring. They didn't understand that we both felt so self-conscious about our height. It's great having Julia to confide in, she makes me feel better.

Ironically my boyfriend's got a complex about his height too. He thinks he's too short and it doesn't help that I'm slightly taller than him. Wes's ambition is to be a fireman. He's 5 foot 7, so hopefully he might still grow taller. I don't really go for tall men, I like the short, stocky type. He always wants me to wear flat shoes or trainers, not high heels, so I'm closer to his height. We've been going out for two years and I've always been taller than him. When we first got together the difference in our height was even more extreme. Then he shot up, but I've carried on growing steadily after the other girls stopped at 13–14. Also I started wearing high heels to cover up the fact that I've got big feet. Wes is always building me up, saying 'You're gorgeous, I'm very proud of you. I don't match up to you, I'm very lucky to be with you.' He's good like that but I think these are pretty typical of the lines that boyfriends use.

My osteopath thinks that I'm still growing. I go to see him because I've got trouble with my hip; the ball clicks in and out of the socket. He tells me not to wear high heels but I ignore him and carry on wearing my high boots. My mum got me a pair of flat loafers, but I wouldn't wear them because they make my feet look like boats. I recently bought a pair of trainers, size 6, although my feet are size 7. They're painful to wear and I've started to develop corns on my toes. If I wear them all day they really make my feet hurt but I love them. They're skating trainers and pretty chunky with a big tongue; the style of them makes my feet look smaller.

I sometimes feel unsteady being tall, mainly because of wearing high-heeled shoes, and worry that I'll topple over. I'm starting a waitressing job next week so I will try to get some nice flat shoes. I've spotted some that I like with open backs but I don't know if I've got the confidence to wear them. I went on holiday to Spain recently and was wearing flip-flops all the time. Normally I wouldn't be seen dead in them for fear of showing off my feet, which are not only big but also not very nice looking; wearing too-tight shoes has given me corns and made my toe joints bend up. Wes came on holiday with me and liked it because I wore flip-flops all the time, so I was closer to his height. I bought the flip-flops when I was there. I saw other girls with large feet wearing them and somehow it was easy to wear them there because I wasn't worrying about people looking at me. It was a relief actually.

Femininity

Jennifer Fisher

I look like a man. I've got men's legs, no boobs and my
body is big, chunky and masculine looking. The only
feminine thing about my appearance is my face and my
long hair.

On holiday the Italian boys were saying I looked like
the footballer Batistuta. I don't know who he is; maybe
he's got long hair, too? I was outraged and shouted
'What? You think I look like a man?' and they just kept
replying 'No, he's a beautiful man' as if that was some
consolation. People say I look Italian; I've got some
Italian blood in me and my hair's dark and my skin olive.
The boys said they liked my legs because they were long.
Maybe they also liked the muscles, which would also
have reminded them of their beloved footballer, but they
didn't mention them. They were admiring my friend
Tasmin's tits, which make her look very feminine and
because mine are really small I felt even more masculine
looking and inadequate. Tasmin has all the luck with
men; she's good-looking, her figure's nice, she's an average

height and she's got lovely breasts. Sometimes I get jealous of the way boys treat her, always rushing to pay for things for her. My other friend Jackie is beautiful, too. I feel worse about myself when I'm with them because they look so much better than me.

Men often find me scary because I'm so big and tall. They just keep saying 'Oh my god, you're so tall!' I don't think they want a tall girlfriend and all the boys I know seem to fancy the smallest girl in the year. I'm taller than most boys and always the tallest girl every year. My friend Summa says boys like short women – 'the best things come in small packages' – but maybe that's because she's short at 5 foot 4.

My height makes me seem older, which might explain why I've been going out with a 19-year-old. I like Tim because he's older than me and when we first got together I was flattered that an older boy would ask me out. He said I was beautiful and had a nice figure. We started having sex when I was 14 and he was 17. I would rather have waited a couple of years but I felt under pressure and didn't want to seem like a little girl. At first I didn't enjoy the sex but then I got into it. After a year I wasn't so self-conscious about my body and showed him my breasts, partly because by that stage I didn't care so much about what he thought. He hasn't got a job and isn't very ambitious; he just hangs around and plays football and fights with his mates. His house is like a youth club, with his friends round all the time. They're jealous of me, slagging me off to him saying I'm rough and ugly, but he ignores them and just wants us to get married and settle down.

When I was growing up I literally kept getting taller and taller and my mum became quite worried. I started my periods early – when I was 11 – and, as I'd already got pretty tall, Mum hoped I would stop growing but I carried on. She decided to take me to the hospital in case I had something wrong with my hormones; every two or three weeks I'd go for blood tests. They were going to give me hormone tablets but then for some reason I got referred to a hospital in Germany. They suggested that we wait and nothing more was said on the matter. Now I've got problems with my knees, which swell up and click and crunch all the time. I think my hamstrings are too short for the length of my thighs so it puts a strain on my knees but the hospital have said they're OK. My mum is pretty tall, she's 5 foot 10 – I don't know much about my dad, my mum was always a single parent – and my 14-year-old brother is 6 foot 1, so it obviously runs in our family.

There are some advantages to being tall; I like the fact that I look older and can get into clubs. I go with Tasmin and Summa who both look older: Tasmin because of her boobs and Summa because she's got a mature face even though she's tiny. I do get complimented on my height. Quite a few other girls have said they would like to be tall like me. Sometimes they're comforting me, other times they really mean it. Summa doesn't seem to like it if I get complimented on my height. The other day we were in the library at school and someone said 'Oh I'd really like to be tall like you.' I think that made her feel inadequate.

I like the fact that I'm slightly taller than Tim. I'm 5 foot 11 and he's 5 foot 10, so I'm more in charge. Other girls have tried to take him away, like in pubs, but I've offered them out and they've backed down. Maybe they think that I'd be stronger than them because of my height.

I've become pretty muscular, especially my legs, because I go to the gym a lot, walk everywhere and do 50 sit-ups and 50 press-ups every night. I do all this exercise because I'm worried about being fat. I weigh 11 stone, which is about 2 stone more than anyone else I know. I must have lead in my bones. My mum keeps going on at me to lose weight and I really try everything I can. I don't eat breakfast or lunch, but this really is the thinnest I can get. Mum has put on so much weight and she regrets it – she doesn't want me to do the same. Now she's quite big on her stomach and hips, but two years ago I was bigger than her, mainly on my thighs, and couldn't fit into her clothes. I think my legs make me look like a gymnast or a body builder and my bottom half is bigger than my top, so I'd love my boobs to be two cup sizes bigger. I asked my boyfriend if he'd pay for me to have a boob job, but he just says my boobs are fine as they are and that I've got nice legs. Boys just don't understand, they don't worry about their looks.

I feel feminine on the inside but the outside lets me down. I'm always trying to make myself look more feminine. I've got long, quite thick hair down to my waist, and it's auburn with red and blonde streaks. I had it permed but it's so long that the perm dropped out and now it's got a slight wave. I wear girlie clothes – skirts all the time, often frilly – and quite a lot of make-up and jewellery. Everything I wear is to try to improve my looks: high shoes to make my feet look smaller and tight tops and padded bras to make my boobs look bigger. If I wear trousers they're sophisticated ones, never sloppy sports clothes or trainers, because I'm worried I'll look more like a man. Summa wears the same types of clothes as me and is always complimenting me on my outfits, but I have disputes with Tasmin and Jackie because they've got into grunga-surf gear and I feel like the odd one out with my feminine clothes. They call me townie because I wear gold jewellery, so I call them grungas.

The most feminine thing about me is my face and I wear loads of make-up; foundation, blusher, eye liner, mascara, lip liner, lip gloss and eye shadow if I'm going out. I won't be seen without my make-up. I want my boyfriend to think I look nice, but most importantly I want my mum, who wears loads of make-up too, to feel proud of me. I look up to her. Even if I'm in all day I'll always dress nicely and do my face and hair. I like to make the best of myself.

Spots!

Kat Hodge

Since my periods started in year seven I have had to deal with spots – without a doubt one of the most repulsive things on this planet. They appear with no prior warning and are guaranteed to pop up at the most inconvenient moments.

My parents are always full of handy tips like 'Don't squeeze them, you'll get scars.' And 'Don't put make-up on them, they'll only get worse.' These pieces of advice have some value but, like most teenagers I know, I choose to ignore my parents' life experience. On the night of a party it's highly unlikely that I'm just going to leave my spots on display so I squeeze and then I conceal. Phew! The horrible thing is gone. Until the next day, that is, when I wake up and look in the mirror. What a surprise, a huge boil has appeared overnight and there is nothing I can do but let nature take its lovely painstakingly slow course. A week before my period and the damn thing swells up again. Except now I haven't just got one to deal with; a whole gang of them have appeared and there is

NO solution. Will they ever go away? I think to myself in a moment of despair when I realise I'm supposed to be going on a date with Lee, the sweetest guy I know, on the very same day.

I get spots when I get my periods, along with really bad period cramps. It isn't even just one type of spot; there are blackheads, whiteheads (pussy), and headless ones, which have to be the most painful. The pus gains pressure underneath your skin but the spot doesn't appear – that is, until a huge eruption takes place. OW! Then it's all over. Blackheads aren't painful and aren't that unsightly if they are small but whiteheads have to be a teenager's worst nightmare. As I walk down the street it feels as if everyone is staring, although it's all paranoia. Undoubtedly the people walking past me are just going about their business shopping or whatever but that's not what it feels like.

I freely admit that I am a victim of advertising – the shampoos, the make-up and the miracle creams that will cure your spots in minutes. Deep down we all know that they don't really work that well, if at all. However, we still stock up on all brands and all kinds of spot-ridding products, from soap to gel to gooey stuff that contains what looks like alien slime but no one really knows what it is or why it's supposed to work. We follow the instructions to the letter, wait fifteen minutes and look in the mirror... nothing. Another fifteen minutes pass and we check again and... still nothing, another couple of pounds and a wasted half hour on another miracle cream that didn't live up to its slogan. If I'm lucky, my skin will be a little less greasy looking but my spots are still there, staring back at me when I look in the mirror.

I've tried out a few natural remedies for my skin. There's a facial scrub you can make by mixing porridge oats with hot water. You rub it all over your face and it takes off the dead skin cells (a tip from my mum). I use it in the wintertime when the porridge is out. Sometimes I get ideas from magazines, although there are disgusting suggestions like putting tomato ketchup or vinegar in your hair – I bet they smell awful. There was a recipe for an avocado face mask with a twist of lime; you leave it on your face for five minutes and then wash it off. It felt very refreshing.

The greasiness on my face is mainly on my nose and cheeks but my forehead is dry so I put moisturiser on every other day. My boyfriend's got combination skin like mine but he won't use moisturising cream; he says it's too girly.

I think boys definitely mind about spots and are less likely to talk to you if you've got them. I'm put off boys who've got serious acne – it's horrible (although my boyfriend's got spots, but they aren't too bad). He uses Oxypads in the morning and at night, which stink of alcohol. Boys seem to be more likely to use these products now because lads are appearing in the adverts. Like when David Beckham was advertising hair gel, it became OK for boys to use it. And now they put loads in their hair, which sets it rock hard and is awful. My brother used to sit there brushing his gel out before he went to bed and it went like dandruff on his shoulders. I don't usually put products in my hair, unless I'm going to a party when I'll smooth it down with styling wax. My hair is perfectly straight but it goes big when I wash it and sometimes has too much volume.

Me and my friends don't talk much about skin and make-up at school, only if we have a sleepover. Then we'll try out different hair styles on each other and use mud masks and take photos of each other looking terrible. We do each other's hair and make-up. Most of my friends don't wear much make-up for school; I only put on lip gloss and a very pale pink natural-looking eyeshadow. I used to put on a lot more make-up – lip liner, lipstick, lipgloss, blusher, bright shades of eye shadow like pink and blue – but never foundation so that my spots could breathe. The make-up was a cover-up for my lack of confidence because I was really nervous when I started secondary school. When you put on make-up you feel like a different person.

My spots were really bad at that time. I was meeting lots of new people and thought they were all staring at my skin rather than looking at me. The friends I hung around with used to take the mickey out of each other a lot. I think we were putting each other down to make ourselves feel better. We'd always be criticising each other, making sarcastic remarks, for instance, about how many bags of crisps were being eaten by a girl who said she was on a diet. In my case it was my spots that got commented on; I got called 'pizza face' and 'join the dots'. We were only joking around but when I thought about it afterwards it felt really vicious. We weren't deliberately trying to upset each other, but because no one said it was getting to them it carried on. I'm sure if I'd said it was upsetting me they would have stopped.

I stopped hanging around with that gang about a year ago and settled in with new friends who didn't slag each other off. I became more confident generally and went to stage school and took singing lessons. I'd sing in school at every opportunity I got: in the choir, at carol services and three of us would write and sing farewell songs for teachers. People started to compliment me on my singing, rather than commenting on my spots.

The spots have started to clear up; there are now fewer of them and I mainly only get them around the time of my period. Besides I don't really have time to be self-conscious now because I'm concentrating on my GCSEs. There were times when I was so paranoid about my spots that if I was walking down the street and I heard anyone laughing I'd think they were laughing at my complexion. I don't feel like this anymore; it's like I'm growing out of them.

Friend

Rosalynne Otoo

Each morning, when I wake up and depending on my mood (often influenced by a once-a-month unwelcome visitor), my body falls into one of the following categories:

1. Ugly body day. This could involve one or several of the following: way too many lumps, bumps and areas of excess fat, too many spots, bags under the eyes big enough to carry Mum's weekly shopping and, of course, the ULTIMATE bad-hair day.
2. Reasonably good enough to go out and face the world day. Pretty much self-explanatory.
3. Wonderful body day. Rare, but occasionally I do feel really great when I stare at my reflection.

Most of the time I get up, look in the mirror and decide that I'm having a reasonable body day. However, today definitely isn't reasonable or wonderful; it's officially an ugly body day.

I'm sprawled on the living-room couch, transfixed by the latest American chat show import. 'Given the opportunity, I would have some work done on myself, but not much,' the guest says, looking down at her body. 'I would probably just have my tum tucked, thighs sucked, upper lip hair plucked, and some fat removed from my rear and put up here.' (The guest indicates her chest region.)

As I listen to this woman confess to all these weird and fascinating methods of achieving the perfect body, I feel strangely interested in what she is saying. I poke at my body currently hidden by layers of sports clothes and breathe a long, drawn out, self-pitying sigh. (I rarely use these clothes for the purpose they were originally intended, ie actually doing some sort of sporting activity, but I own lots, as they are the only clothes I feel completely relaxed in. I'm totally unconcerned when my figure is hidden away under my Adidas sweatshirt and Reebok jogging bottoms.) Watching the screen, I frown in deep thought. If someone were to hand me £10,000 to spend as I wished, I could think of about a million ways to improve my body.

Just as I think this, my grandmother's voice echoes in my mind. 'Improve yourself? What you need to do is eat more. You're all – what's that expression? – skin and bones! It's the food you eat here, full of all those A B C additives and not enough natural goodness. Back home, I'd feed you properly and fatten you up like a baby calf.'

In spite of my present foul mood, I can't help but chuckle to myself. She always manages to make me laugh with her African sayings. Although I'm extremely fond of her, I find it hard to relate to her strong opinions on African culture and don't really take to heart what she says. Maybe it's because I was born in England, and have spent my life surrounded by people of all races. And I have only visited my country of origin, Ghana, a couple of times. Africa seems like a completely parallel universe, where being plump is the norm and being skinny isn't as readily accepted. My parents don't think that a correct body shape exists, so in their eyes I know I'm perfect.

I hear a loud knock at the front door. Without even turning my head I know it's Thania. I shuffle over to open the door, flopping back on the couch. Sometimes it's really hard to see past the green-eyed monster rearing its big ugly head and to remember why she's my friend. The way I see it, I'm the Beast to her Belle, the Hi-Tecs to her Nikes, the frozen home-cooked pizza to her stuffed crust version. In each and every way, I just don't compare. I don't think that it's just my imagination either. I can't even begin to list the amount of times people's eyes glance past me and my frumpy frame and settle on her perfect face, hair and body. We must look like some comedy double act whenever we stand next to each other. With her supermodel stature she has an incredibly unfair advantage over my miniature 5 foot 3. Rapunzel would have killed for her long, rich, thick auburn hair and she has incredibly even skin and rosy cheeks that add just the right amount of colour to her white skin.

I shake myself out of my little daydream as I realise that I'm being spoken to and that she is trying to cheer me up with her kind words. We are going on a huge, empty-our-bank-accounts-of-all-our-money shopping spree. I look up at her stern 'I mean business' face, and resign myself to the fact that I obviously have no choice whatsoever in the matter. I go upstairs to put something a little more presentable on than the sweats I have been living in for the past three days.

'Where do you want to go first?' She waits expectantly for my answer. In my most sarcastic voice I say 'If an ideal world existed, I'd like to be back at home, in my lovely warm bed, as I'm sure that it's mourning my absence.'

'Well you know that's completely out of the question so pick a shop!' she replies in her most cheerful voice.

We go to our favourite shop. The store's bold colours and stylish clothing attract girls like bees to a honey pot and we have to fight our way through the throngs to reach the fitting rooms. We both agree that the mirrors here must be the best in the world. This may sound silly but every time I look into one, I always make sure to send a silent word of thanks to the magic-mirror-making man wherever he may be.

Thania pulls me to face the full-length mirror. 'Tell me what you see,' she says. I glance at my reflection and quickly look down.

'I see a head full of rebellious Afro curls that refuse to do as they are told, a piglet's nose and glasses. My big feet are way out of proportion, my body's too short and to top it all off I've forgotten to shave my legs.'

Thania laughs and shakes her head. 'OK, my turn to tell you what I see. Firstly, I see my best friend. She has flawless cocoa-coloured skin that I would quite happily strangle her for. She has beautiful large brown eyes that tell so much about how she is feeling and perfect teeth to compliment her sunny smile, which lights up any room she walks into. I see a mass of unruly curls that can be turned into any number of amazing styles. I see someone who is actually pretty great and just needs to recognise it.'

It takes my tiny brain a moment to realise she must be talking about me. I start to smile; it's wobbly to begin with, but genuine all the same. And as the happy tears start to well up in my eyes, my pre-period blues start to melt away. The fitting room has just become 100 watts brighter! This time, along with my thank you to the magic-mirror man, I give heartfelt thanks for having such a loyal and understanding friend. Maybe I should abolish ugly body days, and give myself a little more credit.

Beautiful

Emma Collins

My friends call me Pocahontas because I bear a passing resemblance to the cartoon character. I have long dark hair, big brown eyes with flecks of green and a light, coffee-coloured complexion. (I've got a lot of Spanish and a little Barbadian blood in my family from a long time ago.) I am also naturally very slim and have been my entire life.

For years I didn't think I was at all attractive, because of what the girls at school said to me. I just thought I was too thin. Round where I live there are a lot of girls who are big and blonde with blue eyes, the complete opposite to me, so I really stick out. Throughout my time at secondary school I was bullied for being different; mainly for being too thin. I don't know if these girls were jealous of me; my mum told me they were but I just didn't believe her. It got so bad at school that one day when I arrived with a new haircut (like Jennifer Anniston with red highlights), some girls threw yoghurt in my hair. I was about 12 or 13 at the time.

I was called names, like stick insect, Oxfam, lanky, telegraph pole and some people even said that I was anorexic. Just because someone is slim it doesn't mean they have to be anorexic! Also if someone is fat it doesn't have to mean that they ate all the pies. Everyone has a different body structure; that's what makes us all unique and special. My bone structure is small; I'm petite. My mum is also really little and my dad was small when he was young. I've always thought it was something to do with the Spanish blood in us. Why can't people just accept the fact that I'm naturally slim?

It's a myth that men prefer slim women. The men round here always seem to fancy my friends, who are a lot bigger than me. I think they go for at least a size 12 or bigger. I'm a size 8. It wasn't until I was 16 years old and developed a size 32C bust, hips and a bum that men became at all interested in me.

I've always been really active and get bored easily if I'm sitting down for too long. I used to do modern dancing classes at a drama school and loved it so much that I practised moves at home. I was also a member of my local athletics club and ate a lot because you burn it off and you need energy to run. Then I stopped dancing and running because I became so worried about the fact that I needed to put on weight.

Four years ago I became trapped in what felt like hell. I thought that everyone was laughing at me: at my skeleton figure and my hideous looks. I had panic attacks every time I went out. My heart would race, my palms would sweat and eventually I would faint. I was becoming an agoraphobic. Years and years of insults had finally got to me and I gradually got more and more depressed. The last straw was when my grandfather died.

For a year and a half of my life I couldn't go outside my own front door. I was so scared that even if I just lifted my foot over the step I would start violently shaking. I was trapped, a prisoner in my own body. I hated my high cheek bones, my long bony fingers, but most of all I hated being slim. How could anyone ever love someone like me?

My friends and family would say to me 'If you're so unhappy with your weight why don't you try and put some on? Eat more!' But not my parents; they understood. I just could not seem to put any weight on and I felt bad about myself because of what people said.

Eventually I could not even get past my bedroom door. I would just cry, sleep and eat all the time. I was afraid to face the real world with my hideous looks. My coffee-coloured complexion had turned as white as paper and my eyes were sunken. I had not been sleeping properly, because in my dreams people tormented me about my looks and body shape. When I was awake I was having continuous panic attacks, so the doctor prescribed me pills to try to calm me down.

I just wanted it all to end, but then one day a counsellor who had visited me at home came round to take me out of the house and to a clinic for the first time. It was my first time outside for one and a half years. I didn't realise just how much I had actually missed the warmth of the beautiful sunlight on my cheeks, the soft breeze of the wind blowing through my hair and the sweet smell of flowers in the air.

When the counsellor first saw me she gasped. I thought it was because she could not stand the sight of me but she said it was because I was beautiful. The nurse too could not get over the fact that I thought I was repulsive. She told me to take a long, hard look at myself in the mirror and see the person that I really was. All I saw was a lanky skeleton with long straggly hair.

I had to see the counsellor for about six months. She listened to me and told me to write and draw to pour out my emotions, so that she could see what was going on in my head. When I wrote I pushed down hard with the pen because of the anger in me. Slowly she managed to make me break the shell, to make me feel as if I had a new lease of life, a second chance. A chance to love myself and accept who I am. I had thought the depression would last for ever and because I love being active I was bored, trapped in my room. That was one of the reasons that I pulled myself together and asked my mum to go to the doctor to get me a counsellor.

My education had really suffered, so I decided to take my GCSEs at college but I was worried how people there would react when they saw my extremely slim figure. I remember panicking when I noticed a group of boys and girls looking at me and giggling. One of them started walking slowly towards me. I felt a familiar pounding in my heart, dryness in my throat and perspiration on my forehead. Should I run? The boy looked me up and down and smiled shyly and asked me if I would like to join him and his friends. I couldn't believe it; I had been accepted by a group of people. They didn't seem to mind about my size-8 figure. This is when I started to realise that the bullies were the ones with the problem. They tried to put me down because it made them feel better about their bodies and looks.

I was shocked to discover that the people at college found me very attractive. I got paid compliments all the time: 'I love your complexion', 'I wish I had your figure' and 'You are very pretty'. Not at all like the comments I used to get at school: 'I'd rather die than look like you', 'I'd hate to touch you, you might break' and the often repeated 'Do you eat?' At first I felt very embarrassed by the nice comments. I didn't know how to react as I was just not used to getting them but then I got more and more confident.

I never told anybody at college about my struggle to overcome depression and agoraphobia but I still suffer from panic attacks from time to time. Two years ago I still thought nobody would ever love me but now I have met my gorgeous Mr Right. I have proved my bullies wrong by modelling and writing for a local magazine and appearing in local talent shows – in front of an audience. Something I would never have thought possible before.

I managed to pass all my exams at college with high passes. I never had to worry about being called a boffin or a skeleton with brains, because everybody at college just wanted to learn and pass their exams. I am now studying an NVQ in business administration and operating systems, and doing a website design course as well as working in a cybercafé. The course is hard work but I'm really enjoying myself. My bullies have given me the determination to do well in life, because I want to prove them wrong.

Nowadays I'm pleased with my figure but sometimes I still hear comments from people who think I'm too thin. When I was younger the thing that upset me the most was when people asked me if I ate at all. Of course I eat, otherwise I wouldn't have the energy to do anything. I'm always trying to put weight on but it's just not my body type to be fat. I could eat chips every day for a month and still be slim. My goal is to weigh 7 stone but the heaviest I've ever got is just over 6 stone, which is what I weigh at the moment. Now when people ask if I eat I still get a bit upset, but I either choose to ignore the question or say with a confident smile 'Of course I do otherwise I would be dead.' I was surprised when a girl once answered back 'You are so lucky. I wish I was like you.'

Superficial

Claire Sheridan

'You have scars all over your back,' says my friend, shocked, as I bend down to reach something on a low shelf in a shop. I am not surprised when I hear this. Probably because I've heard it before from my pre-pubescent sibling, who I had the job of informing about the joys of growing up and developing stretch marks. When she commented on mine I gave her the sisterly advice 'You'll get them, too.' If she thought I was a freak she had to come to terms with the possibility that one day she might be as well.

So when I hear this for the second time, from my good friend Paul, I'm not surprised. We are out shopping for birthday presents in a novelty gift shop and I have crouched down to examine something inconveniently displayed at ankle level. With my back to him I imagine the shocked expression on his face as he surveys the white, threadlike lines branding the span of my hips. I am wearing rusty-red hipster corduroys and a purple cropped T-shirt, which shows my midriff when I stand normally.

I stand up to say, 'They're not scars, they're stretch marks.' Which isn't entirely true; one of them is a scar from where I had a golf ball-sized lump removed when I was three. 'Everyone has stretch marks,' I preach, partly to soothe my discomfort, because it feels as if my imperfections have been spotlit.

'Not everybody does,' Paul says hotly. 'I don't.'

'No, but your hips didn't suddenly grow when you hit puberty,' I tell him. 'In other words, you're a boy.' Having said that, I've since discovered that boys do get stretch marks, just not so many and not in the same places.

Stretch marks aren't the only imperfection that I've been thinking about lately. I've also been wondering about those little irregularities or freckles that are dotted all over our bodies, branded 'blemishes'. Thinking about blemishes and moles I'm reminded of a documentary about Henry VIII that we watched in a history lesson. It suggested that the king suspected Anne Boleyn of being a witch because she had – along with a third nipple and an extra finger – moles. This struck me as extraordinary; that women should be expected to be smooth all over and if they weren't it was taken as a sign that they had the devil in them. There was no mention that Henry's unattractiveness might have led people to suspect that he was Satan himself. (This probably had something to do with the deadly consequences of such an opinion – I'm sure anyone who dared say that he was ugly would have suffered torture at the very least.) But my point is that women's looks have always been assessed by men, right down to things as small as a beauty spot. Only recently has it started to work the other way, with magazines subjecting men to the same scrutiny that women have put up with for centuries.

I know some girls who also have very particular opinions on the subject of male appeal; for example, a man isn't eligible unless he's at least 5 foot 9. Some of my acquaintances will only go for men who are stunningly attractive, regardless of their personalities, and they've become involved with some really horrible characters. So are girls getting too obsessed by looks, just like men have always been? My boyfriend told me about a girl who was coming on to him at a recent party. She admired him, saying he had 'really nice eyes and a nice mouth'. He then overheard her describing him to his friend as 'gorgeous' and also caught his friend's reply: 'Yes, he is, and he can do really good impressions.' It meant much more to my boyfriend that his friend respected his humour and talent than a woman he didn't know liked him to look at. Or at least that's what he told me!

He feels belittled when he hears that my friends say he's attractive; as if he suspects that they, or I, don't have any respect for him. At the beginning of our relationship he admitted that he worried I had only gone out with him because he was good-looking. I was a little taken aback by his lack of modesty, and a tad offended that he could think that of me. (I was almost tempted to say 'Actually, I don't think you're good looking,' but stopped because it would have been hurtful and untrue.) As for me, I had the opposite insecurity; I felt confident of my intelligence but doubted that I was pretty enough. Maybe he's not that fussy about looks himself; he likes to remind me that he once had a crush on a girl with 'really hairy arms'.

My confidence about my looks probably wasn't helped by the fact that people at school told me I looked like Anne Boleyn (not a reference to any prominent moles or indeed a third nipple but more a comment on the severity of my hairstyle). I used to scrape my hair back into such a tight ponytail that it revealed my high forehead in its entirety. Just like Anne's forehead in the portrait, which was probably considered beautiful at the time. But in these times my forehead won me no such regard. At 13 I was actually just trying to straighten my curly hair, which I hated although others admired it. (Strangely, since then I've cut it short and it's grown back straighter and more manageable, which I regret in a way. I quite like the wild look now.)

Spam was the other remark my forehead generated. This exclamation was accompanied by a slap on my head by the palm of the other person's hand. To begin with when this happened I was indignant and took it as an insult – which I think it was intended to be. But I couldn't think of anything to say in reply and I soon realised why. I had no idea what it meant. I'm still mystified. (If anyone can shed any light on the matter I'd appreciate it; maybe then I'll get the joke.)

More recently I've heard another theory about high foreheads: they can be seen as an indication of heightened mental abilities. A short while ago a friend of mine, possessed of a modest brow, complained about a description she had read of Virginia Woolf that mentioned the writer's intellectually high forehead. So would a person with a narrow portion of skull be described as having an ignorantly low forehead? The description of Virginia Woolf shows us it's still a popular misconception: that the way we look can have any bearing on how well our brains work. A similarly exasperating idea is equating looks with qualities of character. I was annoyed to hear one bloke I know ask another 'Was she nice? What did she look like?' as if being nice and looking nice were the same thing. A girl I knew from school told me that a woman she worked with was 'really nice. She's got blonde hair, and really well-manicured nails.' To me this was no evidence of whether she was nice or not as a person.

To some degree we can change our appearance, and we might imagine we change as people with it. My own personal obsession is my hair, which was shorn and dyed to death in a search to find an image I was happy with. The craziest thing I ever did to it was attempt to iron it straight: my head on one side, hair laid flat across the ironing board with brown paper on top to protect it. Someone else did the ironing for me while watching the telly. The end result wasn't the sleek look I'd aimed at; instead, flat on top, bushy underneath, my hair took on a sort of tent shape.

At the end of the day beauty and hair styles and moles are only skin deep. I think the most important thing is that we feel comfortable inside our own skins.

Identity

Sarah McGarva

When I was 14, I asked my mum if I could get my ears pierced. She said she'd think about it. So, while she deliberated, I went and got my nose done instead.

Reactions to the little silver stud were mixed: my parents went quiet, later admitting they thought it really suited me; teachers raised eyebrows (though they didn't ask me to remove it); and the girls at school divided into two groups, those who were disgusted and those who just wanted to know if it hurt. Six months later, piercings became the height of mainstream fashion and I was devastated.

I was never very happy as a teenager. There were a lot of little reasons bundled together. What it boiled down to was that I wasn't living anything even remotely resembling the life I wanted, and I felt powerless to do anything about it. I didn't want to be attending a tiny school in a pretty (dull) country town in the Scottish Borders. I wanted to be living in the city, where I could go to the cinema, attend concerts, and spend my time exactly as I pleased without the whole neighbourhood knowing about it. But, because I was too young to leave either home or school, I used the only means of self-expression available to me: I dressed as differently as I could.

The other girls at my school dressed to conform. Each seemed a carbon copy of the next: sleek, chin-length blonde hair and inexpertly applied layers of make-up. At school they obediently followed the straight-skirt-white-blouse-red-tie dress code: at home they pulled on blue jeans and tucked in Sweater Shop T-shirts. Even their personalities seemed to come from one standard mould, and I couldn't think of anything more boring.

I wanted to stand out. I wanted to be an individual. I wanted my clothes to display the person I was inside. Colour, comfort and creativity were my priorities. When my frizzy hair became unmanageable, I shaved it off; when it grew back, I dyed it blue and green and purple. In the winter, I swathed myself in layers of T-shirts: granddad top over Nirvana print over close-fitting thermal underwear. My skirts were long and flowing, in bright patchwork, tie-dye and batik prints. My trusty Doc Martens lasted eight years. I was the only person at my school to dress this way, and that made me proud. A few of the teachers made the occasional snide remark, but none of them made any actual attempts to enforce the school uniform, so I chose to simply ignore it.

At a point in my life when I was trying hard to find out who I was as a person, it was important to me to express myself in every way possible. I wasn't trying to be wild and wacky; just making my own decisions independently of popular opinion was enough. When everyone else wanted Nike trainers I wanted Converse boots; even that simple choice marked me as unique. And having the courage to make my own decisions suggested I was strong enough and sure enough of myself to be considered mature and individual, something that was very important to me.

I assumed everyone at school sniggered behind my back and considered me a freak. That didn't bother me; I wasn't happy in their company, and I didn't care what they thought of me. Why they would all want to be the same was beyond me, and I sneered at their lack of originality. I had friends in other classes who thought the same way I did and who supported me, but I was never part of any one group. It can get lonely when you don't have a pack of cronies to protect you. In a country town it is also difficult to meet people outside your own school.

It wasn't until a couple of years later that I received letters from some of the girls I had been at school with, telling me how much they had admired my individuality. I don't know what inspired them to write; probably just nerves about moving to new places. (I left school a year early, so had already been through this.) I didn't realise that a lot of the popular girls felt just as alone as I did, constantly fearing the risk of alienation from their pals. They had been desperate to fit in and too scared to go against the grain, frightened that they would be found to be 'not good enough'. It wasn't until they moved away to study that they found the confidence to be themselves, to start making their own decisions about such simple things as what music to listen to (if any), which books to read and even who to find attractive.

It seems crazy to me that there is so much peer pressure to hide your true personality. I spent my teenage years trying my hardest to define who I was as an individual and to learn to love that person. I found it difficult to understand why anybody would be consciously attempting to mask that individuality and to blend with what was obviously a fairly unforgiving majority, people ready to ostracise one-time friends for nothing more than dressing differently. Though this didn't really happen to me; I was friends with all the other misfits.

My dress sense wasn't just about standing out, it was also about being accepted. I didn't want to be part of the crowd, just like everyone else. I wanted to be myself, but I also wanted people to accept me for who I was: an open-minded, creative individual. I may have dressed differently from everyone in my town but, when I went to Edinburgh at weekends, I found I no longer stood out. When I was there, I loved the fact that nobody stared at me, or tutted their tongues; my colourful dresses stopped being such a big deal. My clothes were an expression of my personality, and they connected me with all the other young people who listened to The Pixies and wanted to be writers or artists or musicians, and just didn't get the appeal of Management Training Courses. Certain people would look at the clothes I was wearing and know all that about me.

My dad resented having felt pushed into a 'socially acceptable' career and lifestyle when he was young. He would have liked to run a pirate radio station or write (he's doing a psychology post-grad degree in LA these days). So he always encouraged my sister and me to think for ourselves. I wore bright clothes expressing that I was a creative person; I was an aspiring writer, into drawing and photography; my comfortable clothes expressed my sense and practicality; a nose stud hinted that I liked grunge music and indie films. It was important to me that people could tell, just from my appearance, that I had bothered to look around and find a style and interests that suited me as a person.

When I moved away to university, this became even more important. Wandering around those first few weeks, a familiar band emblazoned on a T-shirt could be the clue that triggered two complete strangers to approach each other and find a new friend. All anyone knew about anybody else was how they chose to present themselves, and that first impression meant a lot.

I don't believe in judging anyone on their physical appearance. A person's shape, size or complexion will tell you nothing about their character, and to ignore somebody lovely for being overweight, or to hang about with a blithering idiot simply because they're gorgeous, is ridiculous. But it is a fact of life that the first thing we know about a person is usually what they look like, and this can tell us a lot about them.

Nobody can tell from looking at me whether I am nice or nasty, but they can make an educated guess about the music I listen to or the pubs I hang out in. Some will see my frizzy hair and slightly scruffy clothes, and will class me as an unambitious social disaster who will never get to Ibiza – and I don't care, because they're probably right about us having little in common.

Now, at 21, my clothes are no longer the priority they once were. I'm still aware of the signals they are sending out and the impressions they are making. But these days

I am sure of myself and in control of my life. I have chosen my friends, city (Aberdeen), flat and job (projectionist). I am living exactly the life I always wanted and no longer need to put as much emphasis on physical assertions of who I am. I consider myself an intelligent, attractive (and not just physically!) woman, sometimes tactless, but never cruel. I place more value on friendship, pleasure and mental and emotional stimulation than on financial security, material wealth and my social status, and more importance on my values and outlook than on my clothing.

But, as a teenager, clothes were the greatest tool I had. Being a teenager is a time when you are developing a strong identity of your own. When you're not old enough to choose homes or jobs, your choice of clothes and hair style is the clearest way you have to tell the world 'this is who I am'.

Size

Alysse Baldock

I sometimes tell people that I'm not fat, just big boned. This may be the oldest excuse in the book but, after years of anxiety and worrying about my body, I think I may be finally getting to the stage where I believe it myself and have become more comfortable with the shape I am.

It wasn't until I started secondary school and met lots of new girls that I realised that I was large compared to others. In arguments my brother would call me a fat bitch and a pig. He meant these insults as a joke, but there was some truth in them, which made his words more hurtful. I'm the biggest in my family; my brother is tall and thin, my older sister is a smaller version of me and my mum is slender. I put a lot of weight on when I was taking my A levels. I was revising for about ten hours a day and making food that cooked quickly, and buying fast food, so I wouldn't break from studying for too long. I haven't lost all the weight I gained then, and ever since my weight has tended to fluctuate. Most of my friends reassure me I still look good, and that I am naturally larger and maybe big boned, but that's easy for them to say with their slinky size-10 or -12 figures.

It isn't that I'm really fat, I just haven't been blessed with a naturally slender body. To be blunt, I've got chubby arms, a big pot belly and a huge bum. I am what you may diplomatically call a larger woman. And one who doesn't actually enjoy clothes shopping very much. Shopping is supposed to be the ultimate way to cheer a woman up, isn't it? Well, all it does is make me more fed up! Nothing ever seems to fit.

I can blame the shops for only accounting for twigs. Is there really anyone over the age of 10 who fits a size 6? I can blame the manufacturers for making their sizes on the small side. But at the end of the day I still feel like I'm the only one in the world over a size 14.

Once I actually plucked up the courage to ask a shop assistant why the sizes on display are always size 12 and under. She smiled and told me it was because size 14 sells out quickest as it's the average size of women these days. Nice to know, isn't it? If that isn't enough of a pain, I have also been blessed with my family's pear shape, which means my tops are a size 12–14, while my skirts can be anything up to 16, and I can't get a good-fitting dress as a result.

About two years ago I was out shopping for a dress with my friend Gemma. She's a similar shape to me, but taller so she carries her weight better. I was getting quite upset because we'd tried everywhere – Top Shop, Miss Selfridge, Internationale – and I couldn't find anything. I had a bit of money to spend and I just couldn't get rid of it! So Gemma sympathetically suggested we try Evans, which neither of us had ever been to before. I took one look at the displays with large mannequin torsos wearing huge shirts and noticed the skirts folded in half on the hangers so that they wouldn't look so wide, and walked straight out feeling awful.

I still feel resentful when I see thin people on the street, knowing they can buy whatever clothes they want because the high street stores cater more for smaller people. I don't get that degree of freedom; rather than looking at the style of clothes I want, I have to find anything that fits me then see if I like it.

If I'm that unhappy about the way I look, I could exercise or diet, right? Well, yes, but I find diets hard work and exercise is just one of those things I never seem to have time for. Gemma really looks after herself. She eats healthily and does loads of aerobics classes so she's quite toned and looks good – and she enjoys it all. She doesn't force herself to diet, she just enjoys a healthy lifestyle. She's a good role model for me because she's so positive about her body and is always reassuring me about mine.

I recently started a job at a cinema, and when I got my new uniform I had to ask for size 16 trousers, which was embarrassing. Even worse was when I tried them on: I couldn't even get them up my legs. The staff trainer, who was quite small and thin, didn't seem to understand why I was upset. She gave me a size 18 to take home and try on but I could barely do up the zip. I spent about 20 minutes sobbing my heart out. I couldn't even fit into a size people tend to regard as large. I was at my boyfriend Tony's house and he calmed me down by saying that the size system was obviously wrong and not to worry. I later discovered this was true and that many of the girls had trouble with the uniform's trousers in the women's sizes so ended up wearing the men's sizes, which is what I had to do to get a comfortable fit.

Having a boyfriend helps because I'm not worrying about trying to attract someone; my wish is to look good for myself and not to please others. Tony is fantastic. He likes me as I am and says women that are too thin just don't appeal to him. I've never felt embarrassed about showing my body to him. We've been going out for two years and I actually feel comfortable with my body when I'm with him, which has helped me to relax about my appearance. Funnily enough I sometimes feel comfortable with my body anyway. I suppose it depends on my mood and whether I'm going round the shops or not.

I had always wanted my belly button pierced and got it done a few years ago. I swore to myself I'd lose a stone first so I'd have the figure to show it off, and it would be the reward for losing weight. Then, after I'd got it done, I realised I didn't want to show it off. I just thought it looked pretty. I rarely wear short tops or low skirts that show off my piercing, because I am simply not that comfortable bearing my stomach to the whole world. In fact the only people that I've shown it to recently are my little sister and her friends. Amy's only 10 and she thinks I'm really cool with all my piercings. I've got twelve altogether; ten in my ears – six on one side, four on the other – a navel piercing and a nose stud, too. When I visited her recently at my dad's she kept nagging me to lift up my top to show off my navel piercing so that she could impress her little friends.

Now I'm starting to get more concerned about how body image affects younger girls like Amy and my other little sister Holly. I keep reading in the paper stories about

4-year-old girls who cry when they come home from school because their thighs look fat in their school skirt. This is ridiculous; at 4, the only things kids are meant to worry about is falling over and scraping their knees. It's easy to ignore these school kids, thinking of their stories as freak occurrences that don't apply to us or our lives. But these tales are more common than we'd like to think. Just the other day, a friend was telling me her 7-year-old sister had gone on a diet because she thought no one would ever marry her if she was fat!

Where are kids getting their ideas from? Luckily, Amy doesn't seem worried about her shape; she needn't be anyway because she's tall and thin. However, she is getting to the stage where she takes a lot of care with her appearance and has started to be interested in boys. She always spends twenty minutes doing her hair, putting on mousse, gel and hair spray to get it to go straight (although, to be honest, it looks exactly the same when she's finished!). She's very careful when putting on her make-up and probably does it more skilfully than I do! It's funny how things have changed. Her mum and our dad must have relaxed since I was younger because when I used to visit them they didn't like me wearing any make-up at all, and I certainly wouldn't have been allowed to at her age.

I often wonder where ideas of what is preferable appearance-wise come from. Who decides who is fat and who is thin? What I hate is the way people – especially men – voice their opinions so easily. My male friends make comments about the women on telly: who's put on weight, who's lost weight, who's attractive and who's not. Look at all the fuss in the papers because Geri Halliwell lost all that weight. Who cares? I thought she looked better before anyway and now she's got a washboard stomach, so what? And what's the point in making a song and dance about celebrities who lose weight so quickly after giving birth?

The worst thing is admitting to myself the real reason that I am upset by this. It all boils down to vanity, and I would never have dreamed of calling myself a vain person. Every day we are surrounded by body images – in the papers, on the telly, in magazines, and so on – we are meant to aspire to. Nearly all famous, beautiful women in the public eye are thin but, if we don't measure up and are not quite as glamorous, we feel that we are at fault.

We shouldn't forget though that Marilyn Monroe was a size 16 and is still celebrated as one of the sexiest women of recent times. Let's just pray that the larger woman really will come back in fashion, and quick smart!

Footy

Cassia Baldock

Most people's decisions about how they look are ruled by fashion, magazines and peer pressure but the one thing that rules my looks is Liverpool FC. It rules my life; my head, my heart and my body.

I didn't always feel this way. When I was younger I always associated football with the scouse accent, and at school this accent was like nails to a blackboard. It signified nasty little kids who subjected me to their horrible little insults because I dressed differently (in stripy tights, tie-dye skirts and Nirvana T-shirts). I cringe when I recall what I used to wear, but I was judged the height of fashion at the fourth year junior disco in my neon T-shirt, plimsols and bright pink skirt. What the hell; there are too many mistakes and not enough space for shame!

I associated football with scallies, so I certainly didn't want to be a part of it, especially not the image that went with it. There is a picture that best encapsulates what football meant to me: France 1998, England 2 Tunisia 0, and a fat man in Chester cheering and pissing in public.

Yet four days later, during THAT Argentina game in which every England fan experienced both ends of the emotional spectrum, I felt like a fan from birth. I think I realised that not only did I not have to be a certain type of person to like football, but the typical image of the football fan was not exactly right.

A few days ago I was watching a match on TV from the early nineties at the Kop at Anfield. I spotted a very familiar jacket, and something clicked. I remembered a lad from school used to wear that bench coat and my most potent feeling was jealousy. Everyone at school could tell he was a Liverpool fan just by looking at him, and here I am wanting everybody to know exactly how big a fan I am. If Liverpool's new strip consisted of a neon T-shirt, plimsolls and bright pink skirt, I would be wearing it. But the girl in me reminded me that the coat was ugly. Imagine what they would have called me at school if I turned up in DMs, puke-coloured tie-dye tights and a huge red and green bench coat. Weird, probably!

I am reluctantly aware that very few boys would write an article like this. When we go to a match my brother throws on his replica shirt and scarf, and he's good to go. Although, it has to be said, my own little ritual of tying up my hair and putting on a bit of mascara is not dissimilar to him gelling his hair and spraying Brut all over the show. But I realised pretty quickly that replica shirts aren't created with the pear-shaped figure in mind so even the size of my hips has become a factor in my love for Liverpool; something that men wouldn't have to think twice about because the clothes are designed for them (although it is good to see a dress version of the shirts for little girls). Men generally look OK in replica shirts but the only women who look good in them are 'glamour' models. Wearing a skirt with a footy shirt is a definite no-no and peddle-pushers only look alright if your calves don't look like kebabs. Yes, this is the ugly truth!

The point is if you're a real football fan, you're NOT supposed to care about what you look like. You're at the match because of a passion and love for the team and the game. Still, I admit I hated wearing my glasses for a while. Since I've bought a new, more expensive pair, my greater concern now is that I'll forget my glasses one day and not be able to see the game at all. I don't give a flying fig what I look like in them, as long as I can see my boys.

I think I'm desperate to retain some credibility because, if you're plain, you're a real football fan, as you can't be pretty and genuine, can you? I was born blonde, but I've been red or mousy since 14, and I must admit that I'm reluctant to go for highlights because of the stigma: girl + football + bleach blonde = common.

And there's another stigma for girls: whether it's the pert bottoms and firm thighs of the boys on the field or their prowess in the sport that have led us to the terraces. I love Michael Owen because he's a fantastic player and he brings my team, Liverpool, plenty of goals. He diplomatically says in interviews that it's good to see more girls getting into the game, but I wish I had a trophy for every time I've had the third degree from some bloke questioning my real incentives for going to a match! You can't just accuse all girls of jumping on this bandwagon. If all they like about the game is Owen, Redknapp and Beckham, then you are not going to find them forking out twenty-odd pounds for a match. Especially if that money could be spent on make-up and pretty accessories.

But back to me. I know that I can hold my own if I'm challenged about football trivia, simply because I know the facts and figures. There have been blokes chatting to me who are so, like, wowed by my knowledge of the game that they've just got to get my number! And I don't do it to impress them. It'd be good if I could manipulate this to my own means, but it usually turns out that these same blokes are the ones who just won't challenge me, so I end up not respecting them. Football is definitely fashionable right now but it would be rather weird if someone went to all the effort of following the game just to be trendy.

There's no other hobby that dictates your clothing as much as football. You show your colours; the shirt, scarf, hat, bench coat, etc. It really is a uniform. This in fact totally contradicts the direction football has taken. Is there really much unity left in the crowd? From a predominantly male, local, working-class crowd, there is now such immense diversity. It's not even about where you come from anymore and everyone knows the jokes about Manchester United: 'How many Man U fans does it take to change a light bulb? Three: one to change it, one to buy the commemorative shirt, and the other to drive them back to Surrey.' Whoever's attractive will have the biggest fan base, and by this I mean which team holds the greater attraction football-wise and image-wise.

Football's image is veering towards glamour, excitement, superstars and big cash. More women attend the games, and more of the players are modelling, bleaching their flowing locks, appearing in shampoo commercials, wearing skirts and basically acting like a 'bunch of girls'. This is coinciding with the collapse of the old traditions of following football, so no wonder many men have got a bee in their bonnet about women actively following the game. To be fair, though, I know it's not just girls: one lad I know buys football shirts – any shirts at all – because he thinks the colours are really nice.

The culture is still a big part of some father/son relationships, and this is mainly how lads get into it. Live matches are still part of that tradition. I'm glad to say I got into football by my own doing, although I severely regret the many years I've missed out on because I was never taken to matches as a child. Having said that, if my dad had taken me to games, I'd be a Man U fan. Ugh.

With boys and men, you're likely to find that they're just as swayed by the trends and image of football. One particularly body-conscious friend of my brother's was winding him up recently as we were on our way to a match. He was saying he wasn't really interested in buying a replica, but if Armani brought out a slim-fit vintage shirt from the glorious 1970s, he might consider it.

All that said, image in football is not a new thing. Liverpool led the way in Europe in the 1970s, and apparently likewise with style. Keegan's curly perm, anyone?

Proud

Wessen Jazrawi

I'm Iraqi–Irish and over in England to study law at Kent University. I was born in Ireland, my parents are Iraqi and I spent most of my life in the United Arab Emirates, but if you heard my voice you'd think I was American. All of which is a lot less interesting than it sounds!

Most people have no idea where the UAE is so I tend to mention Saudi Arabia to jog their memory. It usually does, with the consequence that they picture a highly restrictive lifestyle, fundamentalist Muslims and extremely hot weather. But it's only the latter that is true. While it is a Muslim country, and the Emirate I lived in forbids alcohol, it is by no means as restrictive as Saudi Arabia, although it becomes more so in Ramadhan, which is a religious festival. Generally, but especially during Ramadhan, women are expected to dress in a modest way. In my family this meant that my father wouldn't like it if I went out in a sleeveless top and would ask me to wear a cardigan, although he wasn't really authoritarian about it. In any case, I didn't want all the attention that you got if you wore immodest clothing; men would stare and women would be disapproving and think you were a slapper. (One of my friends got whipped across her legs by a man for wearing a miniskirt during Ramadhan.) Some of my friends were Muslims and my family generally went along with the system, as it never felt as though things were unbearably restrictive. We watched the same movies, listened to the same music, and invariably were overtaken by the same fads as people the world over.

I have lived in Britain for two years and I don't feel that my perception of my body is any different from other people's here. There are bits I like, and bits I think could do with improving. For instance, I'm fond of my belly but I'm not entirely sure why. I think it looks browner than it should considering that it doesn't get as much exposure to the sun as other parts of me; and it looks browner still when I'm lying down looking at it. I think its colour has something to do with the way that light reflects off it. The rest of me has gone various shades of brown at different times and, when it all fades out, most of me is a golden yellow-brown colour. Except my calves, which also refuse to tan but most people seem to have trouble tanning that part of their body. My belly's not as toned as it could be, to my disappointment. No reason it should be really, considering I do nothing to help it. Besides, I tell myself, if I toned it then stopped exercising, the muscle would turn to fat so I'd regret having built the muscle in the first place. I'm relatively sure this is not true; it's just an excuse to justify my laziness.

There's something indefinably sexy about tummies. Mine is relatively flat and firm but I know that it won't always be, so I may as well enjoy it while it is. There's a certain vulnerability to a tummy, a certain softness despite the firmness, that really appeals to me. Obviously, mine does what all tummies do (I hope): it rolls into mini tyres when I sit down, but somehow that's OK. That's natural, and the little rolls still manage to be cute and squishy and, more importantly, they disappear when I stand up.

One of the reasons I like looking at my tummy is my belly-button ring. I'm fond of it for no apparent reason as it's given me nothing but grief. I've had it for a year and a half but it has only recently stopped exuding gooey stuff. To try to get it to heal I sprayed it twice a day with saline solution and cleaned it with antibacterial soap but it was only when I gave up on all this treatment that it seemed to heal up of its own accord. I'm wondering if part of the reason why it took so long to heal is because the ring is made of steel and I'm allergic to most metals apart from gold. A smarter person would have got rid of it long ago, but it's lucky I didn't as it has now begun to behave.

In a way, it's a silly symbol of leaving home. My mother expressly forbade it; ears were the only acceptable body part to pierce. I had it done a few months after arriving at university. That night, I went out clubbing with my friends and was absolutely horrified to see the number of girls who also had their navels pierced. All of a sudden I was a member of a majority, rather than a minority. I felt like I had just made myself more ordinary, instead of more interesting or sexy.

I think I have attributed sexiness to it although, in reality, it might make no difference to my appearance (especially as most of the time, I'm the only one who knows it's there – the inconvenience of clothes!). I like the glint of steel against my brown skin and it's become a habit of mine to twist it, especially when standing in queues. Quite simply, like my silver anklet, it has become a permanent accessory.

I suppose I'll take it out one day but I haven't really reached that stage yet. I would probably have to be a more settled person, more secure in my sexiness-sans-accessories. Which is really strange, because I've never been hugely into accessories nor have I had any major problems with my body, just little niggling ones, like the waxing, shaving, bleaching, epilating of hair that was clearly placed in all the wrong places just to make my life more difficult. Being Arabic I have more hair than most western women and it's darker, so in addition to removing hair from the usual places, I also sometimes remove it from my forearms. Luckily the hair on my shoulders is blonde and downy so I'm quite happy with it; growing up in the UAE, I've seen a lot worse. My hair is slightly wavy and fly-away. It never has and never will look like it could be from a shampoo ad; it's just not silky smooth enough. I inherited my nose, with almost no modification, from my dad and my sister has an identical one, so I'm not about to get a nose job: family loyalty. It's round and sticks out, dominating my face, which is quite small. Plus, let's face it, I will never be tall.

I sometimes feel that my clothes leave something to be desired. I have certain items of clothing that I absolutely adore, and that automatically make me feel good (like the jeans that I'm currently wearing) but there are others that do little for me. I dress quite casually most of the time, but when I'm dressed and ready to go out, the effect is often not quite what I'd planned. It feels as though something is missing...hang on, I don't look like a model, even though a model wearing these clothes would, well, look like a model! I don't aspire to be one, but I would like to have that certain flair. Someone once said that you should only wear clothes that make you feel good. I suppose that explains why I wear these jeans day in day out!

But, despite all this, there are times when – and believe me I know how much this will sound like heresy – I think I look good. Doesn't it seem ridiculous that people should be uncomfortable with saying they look good? I agree with that song: our bodies are the greatest instrument we will ever own. We should do all we can with them instead of being afraid of what others think; we should be proud of them and flaunt them. Instead of encouraging each other to wear metaphorical T-shirts that say my bum looks big, we should go round encouraging each other to say, damn we look good. Damn, are we sexy! I can't help thinking that would be so much more constructive. It really is crazy how much of sexiness is to do purely with self-esteem. Someone with confidence comes across as being so much more so than someone who keeps subconsciously apologising for their appearance.

I know some would find this patronising, and they might ask what I would know about it. And they'd be right. I've pretty much always been the same size, and that's been thin, or thereabouts. But the fact remains that being thin isn't a requirement of sexiness. It could be said that the few people on TV, in the movies and the media who don't have a size-10 figure have make-up artists, personal assistants, and are dressed in only the finest, so of course they look good. As far as I'm concerned, that's a cop-out. They're sexy because they believe they are. They're confident because they believe in themselves.

I know how corny it sounds, but there is nothing to compare to the pure power of faith: if you don't believe you are good enough, why should anyone else? It's easy to blame someone else. The media portray that this or that is sexy – so it's their fault. And yes, part of it is, of course. But as long as we allow the media to dictate how we feel about ourselves, we're in a bad way. I remember my brother telling me something he heard about girls from Sweden, who were all so gorgeous that no one ever had to be nasty or snobby to anyone else about it, because no one was at all jealous of or superior towards each other. Naturally, I find this hard to believe. It conjures up an image of people all looking very blonde and alike, and I think one of the best things is how different we all are, and how gorgeous we all are in our different ways. The point was that they all believed they were gorgeous and that sounds like more fun.

You can accept you're not perfect and can forever feel that you never look quite as good as the next person; or you can decide you have an amazing body to call your own and create your own style depending on how you really feel. See the beauty in yourself and the world each day. Take responsibility for how you feel. I know which is the cheesier option, but I also know that I'd rather be cheesy and happy, than cynical and unhappy. So go forth and wear T-shirts that say I LOOK SO GOOD I COULD EAT MYSELF.

Contributors' Notes

Ade Atayero is 18 years old and the most amazing girl you'll ever meet. She's into writing, people, travelling, listening to R'n'B, hip hop, soul and a little 'dirty pop'. She's really into her books and is a writer on the side. She is confident, funny, down-to-earth, honest and, by her own reckoning, annoyingly cute. Right now, she's at university studying law which she says is quite cool: 'ignore the stereotypes, law rocks!'

Alysse Baldock (21) is the sister of Cassia, who is also in this book. She has recently finished her degree in Literature, Life and Thought and is taking a year out before pursuing a career in film journalism. Currently, she is working in a local cinema and lives at home with her mother, Carole. Her interests include watching films, writing and spending time with her boyfriend of two years, Tony.

Anna Maffioli is 14 years old and is very busy! When she's not in lessons she's either at the school basketball club, taking the next grade for karate or jamming with her band. She can't wait to pick up her beautiful new electric guitar from the shop and has begun to write a lot of song lyrics, which she is going to put to music for her band. She loves listening to music and chatting on MSN with her friends and is starting to skateboard again. She has a great life at home and really enjoys everything she does.

Cassia Baldock is 23 and the sister of Alysse. She is still trying to figure out what she wants to be when she grows up. In the meantime, her priorities in life are football, music, going out, writing and creating colourful characters for her website. Having spent so much energy trying to get work published she figured that by creating her own website she would at last have enough space to run amok in. Originally from Merseyside, moving to London hasn't interrupted her passion for football and Liverpool FC – although current ticket prices are doing their best. She's therefore added to her love of Liverpool by following the mighty Brentford FC.

Claire Sheridan is 19 years old and a first-year student at University College London, studying English. During her gap year she volunteered part-time for the London Wildlife Trust, and has just written about the experience in their newsletter, *Wildlife Network*. In her spare time she sketches surreal cartoons which only her friends and family seem to appreciate, listens to 'alternative' music or cheesy '70s stuff, attempts to play the piano and saxophone (not both at once) and watches films avidly. She is a vegetarian and has her nose pierced.

Emma Collins (also known as Pocohontas) is 18 years old and is now living with Simon (her partner) in Hampshire. She works as a trainee computer technician in a local cybercafé. She is also very involved with *Rant*, a local youth magazine, both writing and modelling. She is comfortable with the way she looks now and doesn't stand for abuse anymore. She plans to live her life to the full and would just like to say a big thank you to everyone who helped her beat her depression.

Esther Linton is 24 years old and lives with her sister who is more of a best friend really. She works in a hospital as an occupational therapy assistant – she's always loved caring for people and has worked in nursing homes, for people with learning disabilities and done community work. She thinks the best qualification you could ever get is life experience. She comes from a fairly big family and has one younger brother, two older sisters and one older brother, all with different jobs and visions. She loves them very dearly. She likes to do yoga and is beginning to get more interested in alternative therapies, having recently completed an Indian head massage course which was very relaxing. She likes to do different things which are fun and interesting and she hopes to do a skydive at some stage. At the moment she's single and enjoying her journey in life.

Fatima Patel, aged 20, lives in the busy city of London. She's currently studying Accounting and Finance at university, and in between studying hard she likes to read as many books as she can get her hands on, watch *Buffy the Vampire Slayer* and *Angel* religiously and listen to music. She's quite mischevious and loves playing practical jokes on her sisters and brother.

Gemma Wilkins is 19 years old and currently at university studying for an HND in professional writing. She enjoys comedy and horror films and is a devoted follower of 'The Rocky Horror Picture Show' and stand-up comedians. She loves heavy metal, especially Metallica and Alice Cooper, but also enjoys '80s New Romantics and '70s glam rock. In her spare time she plays the drums, and can usually be found out and about with her boyfriend and friends, or adding to her ever-expanding collection of bears.

Jackie Harris is 15 and friends with Jennifer and Tasmin who are also in this book. She can be extremely shy when you first meet her so you might think that she's sweet and quiet but her sense of humour is a big part of her personality. She lives in Hastings and works on the till in the same café as Tasmin in her spare time. She loves going to Brighton and hopes to go to college to study media or English. She is very into hip hop and R'n'B and can't stand dance music or anything with a repetitive beat.

Jennifer Fisher is 16 and is friends with Tasmin and Jackie. She loves shopping for clothes, and gets a real kick when she can actually find something that fits her. She loves painting and sculpture and would like to be a fashion designer when she gets older. She's into DMX, R'n'B and garage, and loves sleeping and Italian food, especially lasagne.

Kat Hodge is 15 years old and lives with her mum, dad and older annoyance or brother, Robin. She likes school (but says she's not a freak!), socialising and music. She listens to rock and nu-metal bands such as Linkin Park, Staind, and Limp Bizkit. She's also into singing in a big way, although not the type of singing you would associate with the bands she's mentioned. She's an R'n'B singer in a group called Rough Silk and she regularly sings at school events. Drama is her favourite subject because it's really the only subject that gives her freedom to do what she wants. She's planning to be a journalist or editor of some sort in the future, after college and uni of course. Her favourite people in the world have to be her friends and boyfriend (Michael) who she always goes out with at weekends, usually to Camden market or the cinema, and who have been known to have wild parties. Her best friends Claire and Tesni keep her sane and she loves them to bits.

Lucy Parkin is 19 and currently enjoying a year out before taking up a place at Oxford to do Psychology next year. She likes to set herself challenges, writing being one. Her latest is a six-month voluntary project in Ecuador which she's both looking forward to and dreading at the same time! She enjoys spending time with her friends, drinking red wine and laughing – generally having fun is high on her agenda along with achieving the best she possibly can. She likes to see the good in people and hopes that they can return the favour.

Melissa Reardon is 23 and the oldest of four fantastic children. She is currently living in Bristol and temping while taking time to work out a cunning plan to move back to the centre of the universe (aka London) for all the amazing gigs and clubs. She worships the Manics. Music was her first love, and it will be her last! When she grows up she wants to be famous; until then she's playing at being the ultimate messed-up rock chick.

Rosalynne Otoo is 17 and is currently studying for her A levels in English Literature, Geography and Sociology. She loves to read all sorts of books and to listen to R'n'B music at an (almost) deafening level. Rosalynne also tries to have as much fun as possible when socialising with her friends by going to restaurants, and to the cinema, to name a few activities. When she isn't living the life of a typical layabout student, Rosalynne takes part in some voluntary work with the local group of Jehovah's Witnesses. After the sixth form, she hopes (and prays) to go onto university to study English literature. She's a comedian and loves telling jokes. Rosalynne would like to dedicate this story to her friend Ian.

Sam Lyon is 17 and currently embracing the freedom of college life. She isn't alone anymore but is surrounded by good friends. She is taking a psychology A level in the hope that one day she may be able to help other people through similar experiences with eating disorders. She loves reading French and Russian literature and is a huge fan of indie music and modern art, like Dali and most of the stuff at the Tate Modern. She isn't skinny anymore, but proportioned and slim, and will proudly admit to being quite pretty. Despite the fact that living with her eating disorder was not a great experience in itself, she learnt a great deal about herself during that time.

Sarah McGarva is 23 and lives in Aberdeen, where she works as a projectionist. When she is not watching films for free, she hangs out with her friends, reads, dances fairly badly, and sulks about not having received any text messages for at least 40 minutes! She is all set to take the literary world by storm with her critically acclaimed novels and short stories, although it has been pointed out to her that she might actually have to write them first.

Susie Nathan is 23 and has always lived in London, apart from a brief sojourn in Liverpool. She has been writing for pleasure since her early teens, but for years was too afraid to show it to anyone, until a teacher convinced her to apply to a Creative Writing degree course at John Moores University. In her spare time she writes about issues that affect contemporary society, pieces that (she hopes) will make people laugh, cry and keep on reading. Someone once said her writing was like having an intimate chat with your best friend. Recently, she has taken an interest in writing for the big screen. Her other interests include music, film, digital photography, surfing the internet and holidays in obscure places. Currently she is attempting to direct a video for a London-based hip hop collective, but has found it harder than she first thought and will probably stick to writing!

Tasmin Smith is 16 and friends with Jackie and Jennifer who are also in this book. She is extremely outgoing, loves being social and meeting new people, and seems to know absolutely everyone! She has lots of goals and can hold extremely in-depth discussions and debates. Her only fault is having huge obsessions with boys, which seem to last a lifetime, until she moves onto her next victim! Tasmin is very into music, which she claims to be an essential asset in looking for prospective boyfriend material, and especially likes bands such as REM and Red Hot Chili Peppers. In her spare time she works in a café.

Wessen Jazrawi, aged 20, is a final-year law student at the University of Kent, and is still enjoying the course. She is planning to take her Legal Practice Course, which she needs to do to become a solicitor, next year. Then she's going travelling, taking in South America, Canada and maybe Australia and New Zealand – she can't wait! She spends a good deal of her spare time devouring TV soaps. In her opinion, *Neighbours* and *EastEnders* are great instant ice-breakers as everyone watches them. She enjoys television, good books and chocolate in equal measure.

Resources

Brook
Tel 0800 0185 023
Advice for the under 25s on contraception, pregnancy and sexual health.

Childline
Tel 0800 1111
Telephone support and advice for all children and young people. (Calls are free.)

Eating Disorders Association
103 Prince of Wales Road
Norwich
NR1 1DW
Tel (Admin) 0870 770 3256
www.edauk.com
Provides telephone support and written information for people with eating disorders and their friends and family.

Youthline Helpline 01603 765 050, 4pm–6.30pm (weekdays)
Can call you back to save your phone bill.

Adult Helpline for people over 18, 01603 621 414, 9am–6.30pm (weekdays)

Talkback, a magazine for young people. Send a large stamped addressed envelope for a free copy.

A cheap range of leaflets are also available (eg *Eating Disorders in Young People*) which include information on how to get help (cost 60p).

First Steps to Freedom
Tel 01926 851 608
Telephone advice and counselling for anyone with eating disorders, anxieties and phobias. All volunteers on the helpline are ex-sufferers themselves.

Get Connected
Tel 0808 808 4994
admin@getconnected.org.uk
A helpline for young people. Can help you find the best source of help, whatever the subject. (Calls are free.)

National Drugs Helpline
Tel 0800 77 66 00
24-hour telephone support.

National Self-harm Network
Tel 020 7916 5472

Overeaters Anonymous
Tel 07000 784 985

Samaritans
Tel 0845 790 9090
24-hour telephone support.

www.something-fishy.org
A very useful US website for people with eating disorders.

Youth Access
Tel 020 8772 9900
Service for 13–25-year-olds. Will give you telephone numbers for local services that provide information, advice and counselling.

Youth to Youth
Tel 020 8896 3675
help@youth2youth.co.uk
www.youth2youth.co.uk
Open Monday and Thursday 6.30–9.30pm. All volunteers on the phoneline are aged between 16 and 21 and are trained to provide support to under 19s with emotional difficulties.

Alison Hadley of Brook Advisory Centres, editor
Tough Choices
Young Women Talk About Pregnancy

Recommended by Brook Advisory Centres

'I had a gut feeling that I was pregnant. I confided in my best friend and we decided to get a pregnancy test after school. I was so scared waiting for the result. The two blue lines confirmed my worst nightmare – I was pregnant.'

What would you do if you found yourself pregnant unexpectedly? Would you keep the baby, put it up for adoption or opt for a termination? And what about parents, friends, school? Could you rely on your best friend to keep a secret? Where would you turn for help and advice? What would life be like with a new baby? In this moving and powerful collection, young women share the difficult choices they've made, and reflect on how their pregnancy affected their lives – from dealing with the emotional consequences of a termination, to the joys and tribulations of being a young mother. A riveting, thought-provoking and compelling read, *Tough Choices* gives a powerful insight into teenage pregnancy.

Non-fiction: £4.99
ISBN: 0 7043 4953 1